SCOTLAND

The Cuillins, Skye

SCOTLAND
Ena MacPherson

CONTENTS

Published by Collins
Glasgow and London
First published 1967
Revised edition 1977
Reprinted 1977

*Cover photograph of Kilchurn Castle, Loch
Awe is reproduced by permission of
J. Allan Cash Ltd*

Maps by Broad Oak Studios

Drawings by Ian Harley

*Photographs by courtesy of
A. D. S. MacPherson (title page)
Scottish Tourist Board (pages 8, 11 top and
bottom, 16, 33 bottom, 44, 52 bottom)
Scottish Field (pages 33 top, 39, 43)
Dept. of the Environment (page 49 bottom)*

ISBN 0 00 435746 9

INTRODUCTION

Neither the tourist amenities of Scotland nor the beautiful scenery nor the weather will ultimately determine whether you enjoy your holiday in 'the land that likes to be visited'—it is up to you. Whether you intend spending a few days at the Edinburgh Festival, steeping yourself in cultural activities, or a week camping in Wester Ross, remember that, before all else, you are on holiday. You are breaking away from your everyday pursuits and surroundings, so do it thoroughly. Leave your preconceived ideas behind: come to Scotland with an open mind and a sense of adventure, and you will be amply rewarded.

With a population of just over 5 million, Scotland covers 75,327 sq km (29,795 sq ml), exclusive of its lochs and rivers, and offers every variety of scenery from the Northern Highlands which include the highest mountain in the British Isles (Ben Nevis, 1343 m/4406 ft) to the heavy industrial area around the Clyde, the horizon broken by the silhouettes of innumerable cranes and the masts of ships from all over the world. New towns like Cumbernauld and East Kilbride, engineering feats like the Forth Road Bridge with a single span of 1005 m (3300 ft) or the nuclear generating station at Hunterston, modern universities like Strathclyde and Stirling are unexpected features in a country chiefly known for the beauty of its lochs, mountains and glens, the ancient universities of Edinburgh and St Andrews, its outstanding golf courses and fast growing winter sports centres. No visitor can hope to see more than a fraction of Scotland on a brief holiday, but the country can be conveniently divided into areas which may be covered in a fortnight.

Edinburgh, Fife and the Borders

This section of Scotland encompasses a centre of high population and, in Edinburgh, one of the most beautiful capital cities of the world, some of the loneliest areas (the gentle, rolling sheep country of the Borders) and one of Scotland's least attractive areas—the industrialized part of West Fife.

No part of Scotland is easier to reach. All roads lead to Edinburgh, and from there either trains or bus services and good motoring roads radiate to all corners of Fife and the Borders. A major attraction is the visually exciting, modern road bridge across the Firth of Forth, side by side with the older (1889) but still impressive railway bridge.

Each of these areas conjures up a separate mental picture—the rich agricultural country of the Lothians and its quaint, quiet villages; Fife, that odd mixture of ancient and modern. The ancient Kingdom of Fife is represented by St Andrews, Culross and the East Neuk fishing villages, yet only a short distance away is Glenrothes, a new town still in the process of settling down and finding its own identity. And the Borders conjure up soft, rolling countryside, Saturday crowds yelling enthusiastically for the local Rugby team, and the contrasting stillness of the Border Abbeys.

There is little high drama in the Lowland scene but plenty of variety, and with Edinburgh as a base, it can be seen in comfort and ease.

Glasgow and the Southwest

Glasgow is the centre of a great network of transport serving its immediate neighbourhood, Loch Lomond, the Clyde coast and the southwest of Scotland. The coastal steamers are speedy and efficient, and make even the most prosaic of journeys around the Clyde a holiday affair.

The area is split into two quite separate parts—the first part covers Glasgow and the Clyde coastal area of trim, bustling and carefree resorts. The distinctive accent of Glasgow and the unaffected friendliness hit the visitor like a slap on the back. This is Scotland at its most uninhibited with its fanatical football supporters and its crowded pubs, designed for solid drinking. The other part, the southerly half, is the rather reserved area of Dumfries and Galloway where a quieter, slower pace commands. This is perfect country for the motorist who likes to meander along good, uncrowded roads, who prefers the undramatic but infinitely more tranquil in scenery.

If you do not want a large city as a base, try Dunoon or Rothesay for the Clyde coast, and Kirkcudbright for the quieter Galloway district. Prestwick is an attractive centre from which to explore both areas.

Central Scotland

This is probably the area of widest overall appeal for the visitor. Some like the douceness of the Borders, others the stark grandeur of the northwest, but everyone loves Perthshire in central Scotland. Part of its appeal lies in its accessibility—Pitlochry is an ideal centre—part in the variety of activities it can offer. Visitors, experienced or not, can ski in winter (occasionally to the end of May), pony trek, walk, fish or climb in summer. They can tour the beautiful Trossachs area where the hills have no exceptional height, yet have the majesty of the great mountains of the north, softened by wooded, rugged lower slopes that sweep down to graceful blue lochs.

The area encompasses the great Cairngorm mountain range with its bracelet of lively little towns all eager for visitors. Glenmore Forest Park near Aviemore and Nethybridge is ideal for children: just tracts of rugged ground, mountains behind, a loch (Loch Morlich) in the centre, and a herd of reindeer—an experimental herd introduced from Lapland—roaming free in one part. Permission to visit the herd can be obtained from the guardian, Mikel Utsi, whose house stands in the forest park. If the season is right, your hotel may be able to arrange it for you.

It is in this area, too, that you will find the only lake in Scotland, the Lake of Menteith (all the others are called 'loch'). On Inchmahome Island stand the remains of a 13th-century priory which can be visited by boat from the Port of Menteith. Mary Queen of Scots, when a child, was smuggled from Stirling and kept at Inchmahome for a short while before being sent to France.

Central Scotland, full of history, full of natural beauty, can be seen comfortably from several centres including Stirling, Crieff, Perth and Pitlochry.

The Northeast

The Northeast, from Nairn down to Dundee, includes that great eastern bulge of Scotland, an area of good farming land, the home of the famous Aberdeen-Angus cattle, and the honest-to-goodness fishing ports. Aberdeen rightly dominates the area, not only as chief port on the eastern coast and its more recent fame as the business centre of the off-shore oil industry, but as the nearest city, rail centre and airport for Royal Deeside, that remarkable tourist attraction popularized by Queen Victoria, which takes in the towns along the River Dee from Aberdeen to Ballater, Braemar and Balmoral.

West of Scotland

The West of Scotland is beautiful, wildly romantic and accessible. Oban is the ideal centre, but Fort William is also well placed and is the starting point of the most beautiful railway journey in the country—the West Highland line from Fort William to Mallaig. This is one trip that is worth any visitor's time and money, and although there is a road running parallel with the railway, one has more leisure to enjoy the majestic scenery from the train. But like many of the railway lines in Scotland there is always the possibility of closure, so do check that it is still running before you finalize your plans.

Some of the finest mountain scenery in the West surrounds the village of Ballachulish, but the whole area is a treasure chest for those seeking a quiet village, shapely lochs and trips to the Inner Hebrides.

The Hebrides

The Hebrides are too often ignored by visitors from abroad, but the small effort involved in catching a boat at Oban or Mallaig offers ample reward in revealing an aspect of Scotland which it is impossible to see on the mainland. The Hebrides put the rest of Scotland into perspective. They are the ultimate haven for those harassed by traffic problems, commercialism and congestion of their everyday lives. Time goes a long way out there, and one of the best ways to visit the islands is by hiring a sailing boat. The Scottish Sports Council (address on p. 35) will supply full details.

It is difficult to recommend one particular island, but perhaps Iona and Barra should be tried first. Three days is all you need for each— you might like to visit an island after a week based on Oban. Do not take your car if you really want to absorb the atmosphere of the Outer Isles, although there are car ferries operating to both Harris and North Uist. Caledonian Macbrayne Ltd (address on p. 34), operates a 4-day tour covering most of the islands including Skye, but it is more fun to organize it yourself. The following tour will enable you to see more and to relax more.

From Stornoway (Lewis), reached by boat or plane, take a bus to Tarbert (Harris) where you should stay at least long enough to take

the same bus round Harris to Rodel in the south, Leverburgh and back to Tarbert. A boat will take you to Lochmaddy (North Uist), and a local bus continues down the island, across a causeway to Benbecula, across a causeway to South Uist and down to Lochboisdale. There you can make a brief trip to Eriskay by mail boat before taking a steamer to Castlebay (Barra), whence you can return to Oban by boat via Tiree, Coll and Tobermory on Mull, or fly from the cocklestrand near North Bay on Barra direct to Abbotsinch (Glasgow).

The North, Orkney and Shetland

This is the area of high drama, of a mountain rising up out of nowhere in solitary splendour, as does Suilven near Lochinver, of a sandy bay girdled in silence by rocky headlands, far removed from the crowded beaches we call resorts. This is the home of simple kindly people who live by the land and the sea, who still have time to talk to a neighbour, to help a stranger, and who still retain the ability to make their own entertainment.

Here, Nature is master. The air is clean. The colouring is true. And if you are a city dweller who has forgotten the exhilaration these things bring, drive straight to the north, for these pleasures are precious, and few areas like this are left in Europe.

Orkney and Shetland are both large complexes of small islands scattered like the ocean spray across the North Sea. Remote, closer to Norway than they are to southern Scotland, they are readily accessible by sea or air and seem very much nearer since Shetland especially has become a major centre of the oil explorations.

THE PEOPLE

The Scots see themselves as sturdy, honest and forthright. They have no desire to be classed with the English who, for them, are a separate race. Scots consider that the English talk too much, and it does seem that the farther north one goes, the less people talk about trivialities. But Lowland Scots, from the densely populated area of the country, are much like people from any part of Britain. A Lanarkshire miner has a lot in common with a miner from the north of England, and both will have much in common with a miner from Wales. But the farther north you move, the greater will be the difference in temperament.

The Highlander, in so far as it is safe to generalize, has a ready sense of hospitality, a pawky sense of humour and a natural shyness with strangers. Never make the mistake of believing your arrival has gone unnoticed. In a remote village everyone knows when a stranger has arrived, and everyone is intensely curious about him, though no one will be so ill-mannered as to question him directly, but people will appreciate any personal information you may care to volunteer.

If you are travelling in the far northwest or around the more isolated Hebrides, it is easy to imagine yourself cut off from civilization, but do not succumb to the temptation of regarding the local inhabitants as lost souls who know nothing of life in the big world. A great reverence for education and a pioneering spirit have made the Scots into some of the best sailors, bridge builders, ministers and teachers roaming the world today.

The Clan System

Clans rightly belong to the Highlands where settlements were small and scattered. The people of a settlement, by nature warlike, inter-married and thus everyone was related to everyone else. Ruling over this large family was a chief to whom everyone gave his loyalty. Loyalty was fierce, and a chief would fight as bravely for the lowliest member of his clan, and vice versa, as he would for his own son. Cattle and sheep were never safe from neighbouring clansmen, and clan warfare was accepted as natural and inevitable.

To distinguish one's kinsmen, the clan tartan was worn as a kind of uniform. The actual costume was the kilt, at once simple and amazingly intricate. Simple because it consisted of a skirt and a kind of portable blanket; intricate because the tartan is designed in a series of squares, each square of the pattern being called a 'sett', which had to be displayed intact.

There were two kinds of kilt. The *feileadh beg* (little kilt) is the original of what is worn today, sewn into pleats with an apron front and straps at the waist. The *feileadh mor* (plaid) was a length of some 5 m (16 ft) of tartan, half of which was folded around the body by hand to show the setts, and the remainder thrown over the shoulder where it was pinned by a brooch. This kilt was held at the waist by a broad belt.

In 1746 after the defeat of Scotland at the Battle of Culloden, the kilt and the tartan were banned by the Hanoverian Government. Six months' imprisonment was the penalty for anyone caught wearing the kilt, a second offence meant deportation for seven years. Two generations of Scots were forced to adopt trousers before the ban was lifted in 1782, although tartan trews had long been worn by the more distinguished members of the clan who owned a horse and found a kilt unsuitable for riding. A memorial to this ignominious ban still exists today in the dance called 'Seann Truibhas' (Old Trews) which is performed at Highland Gatherings. It was a fitting expression of the Highlanders' disgust at the English mode of dress—an expression they could not be imprisoned for.

Sunday in Scotland

In Glasgow and the Galloway area almost 50% of the population is of Catholic faith, largely from Ireland, although there is a Highland element. The other main church is the Church of Scotland, which is essentially Calvinistic, but in the North and West the Free Church of Scotland is very strong and in certain areas such as Skye or North Uist one is expected to behave very circumspectly and respect the Sabbath. Conversely South Uist and Barra for example, and certain Highland areas, are still Catholic because the Reformation never penetrated there.

It is worth bearing these facts in mind, for Sunday in Scotland, by and large, is still regarded as a day of rest. Shops are closed and only in the large cities will you find restaurants open, though hotels will always provide meals. Many Highland garages close on Sundays, and filling stations are few and far between, so keep your tank full.

Few trains run in the Highlands on Sundays. In central Scotland there are more, but stations may be staffed only for the half hour before arrival of a train, if it is the only one running that day.

Although a limited number of restaurants and public houses have '7-day licences', most of the public houses are closed, and you will have to go to a hotel for a drink.

LANGUAGE

Should you be in the north-west Highlands and Islands you will be struck by the distinctive lilt of the English spoken there. The explanation is that English—especially in the Islands—is not the first language of the people but rather Gaelic, the ancient Celtic language once spoken over most of Scotland but now confined as a daily speech to these areas of the Highlands and Islands. Despite its decline over the last hundred years, there has been a recent upsurge in interest both in the language and the rich heritage of music and song associated with it and these are featured at the National and Local Mods—cultural festivals—held each year in many parts of the Highlands and Islands. Information about all aspects of Gaelic language and culture can be had from Abertarff House, Exhibition and Sales Centre, the Headquarters of the Highland Association in Inverness. The Association also has an office in Stornoway, Isle of Lewis. Look for notices about Ceilidhs—evenings of Gaelic song and music and dance—the Ceilidh is a feature of Highland entertainment in many areas throughout the summer months where you have a chance to savour the authentic Highlands.

Not even the Scottish Tourist Board would claim that Scotland has perfect weather. But snowy winters favour the winter sports enthusiasts and a good drizzle of rain keeps the fishermen happy. The rest of us must choose carefully. May is frequently a most agreeable month on the west coast of Scotland, and for any of the Hebridean islands (and this includes Skye) it is the best choice. May is beautiful, too, in Perthshire. The russet leaves of last autumn still pile deep in the woodlands around Pitlochry when the trees are already bursting with new greenery.

But the other great period of glory for Scotland is autumn—from the end of August and well into October—when the heather is purple on the hills and the trees and bracken mix with it in golden relief.

If you feel the cold take the precaution of packing a hot water bottle, and always travel with a warm sweater, a nylon raincoat (one which folds into pocket size) and stout shoes for walking. Even if you intend breathing no more fresh air than you will get pulling a bunch of heather, the shoes will be useful.

You will find that a tweed skirt and sweater are acceptable all day long in small hotels, and one plain dress for dinner will make you feel more relaxed after a day in the open air. Unless you are staying in a city or a very large and expensive hotel like *Gleneagles* or *Turnberry,* evening dress will be unnecessary. The current vogue for casual evening wear means, however, that a long skirt is acceptable anywhere for dinner.

CURRENCY

There are currently 5 banks in Scotland which are entitled to issue bank notes of their own design. These are, strictly speaking, not legal tender in the rest of the British Isles, you may have difficulty exchanging them, and you should ensure that you have only Bank of England notes with you before going south of the border. Banking hours are Monday to Friday from 09.30 to 12.30 and from 13.30 to 15.30. On Thursdays most banks are also open from 16.30 to 18.00 and at Friday lunchtimes. Banks do not open on Saturday or Sunday.

TRANSPORT

By Air Scotland is readily accessible from most parts of the British Isles. British Airways and British Caledonian fly into Edinburgh, Glasgow (Abbotsinch), Aberdeen and Inverness. The London/Glasgow and London/Edinburgh BA routes are shuttle services (which means

13

you don't have to book in advance, simply buy your ticket before boarding the plane). There are also regular flights to and from Belfast.

Within Scotland there are regular and frequent flights to Edinburgh, Glasgow, Aberdeen, Inverness, Wick, Campbeltown, Orkney, Fair Isle, Shetland (since the advent of oil it is better to book this particular route well in advance), Dundee, Dornoch, Skye, Oban, Barra, Islay, Benbecula and Stornoway. Loganair (the Glasgow-based airline owned by the Royal Bank of Scotland) who run some of these domestic connections also do charter work for those who want to get somewhere quickly.

By Train There is a wide choice of fast trains from all parts of the British Isles (connecting with steamer services from Ireland where appropriate) to the main centres, as well as several sleeper services. Fast electric services (5 hr) from London to Glasgow and (5¼ hr) from London to Edinburgh have cut out much of the dreariness of these particular routes. Meals are available on most long distance trains, but always check first. British Rail operate a package holiday programme for those who would like to book their accommodation at the same time as their transportation. The Golden Rail brochure is available from travel agencies or direct from Golden Rail (address on p. 35).

Scotland's railway lines are among the world's most beautiful. Modernization has involved the cutting of many attractive routes, but two especially beautiful ones may still be enjoyed. These are:

Waverley

Inverness across the country to Kyle of Lochalsh, whence steamers leave for Skye; the West Highland route from Fort William to Mallaig, a trip so beautiful that it is worth planning your whole visit around it.

A large number of the Clyde coast resorts are served by fast diesel services from Glasgow which connect with the Clyde coastal steamers. Special rail/steamer fares operate on these routes, and information leaflets are available at all railway stations or from some of the useful addresses on pp. 34–5. There are steamers on Loch Lomond and Loch Katrine, and combined rail/coach/steamer trips make excellent outings to these famous beauty spots.

British Rail offers 7- and 14-day unlimited travel tickets ('Freedom of Scotland' tickets) at considerably reduced rates for those who want to cover large areas by rail, as well as a large selection of weekend and special excursion tickets during the tourist season.

By Boat Greenock, near Glasgow, is Scotland's main intercontinental port, but there are direct trans-Atlantic services only from Montreal and Quebec. It is possible, however, to sail from New York to Cobh (Ireland) before moving on to Scotland. From Ireland there are services from Larne to Stranraer and Larne to Cairnryan.

There are good connections between the mainland—principally Oban, Mallaig and Kyle of Lochalsh—and the Western Isles. These boats run all the year round, and carry mail and vital supplies as well as passengers.

TO THE MEMORY OF
WILLIAM MILLER,
THE LAUREATE OF THE NURSERY
AUTHOR OF WEE WILLIE WINKIE
BORN IN GLASGOW AUGUST 18..
DIED 20 AUGUST 1872

Services to the Orkney and Shetland islands are run by the North of Scotland, Orkney & Shetland Shipping Co Ltd, Matthew's Quay, Aberdeen. This is an excellent service from Scrabster (Caithness) to Stromness (Orkney) and from Aberdeen to Kirkwall (Orkney) and Lerwick (Shetland), and the round trip itself makes an enjoyable and inexpensive holiday for the enthusiastic sailor. It is usually better to travel tourist class, as first class accommodation is normally more heavily booked. See also IF YOU ARE MOTORING.

By Coach A regular coach service runs from London to Edinburgh and London to Glasgow; it is the cheapest way of making either journey and can be done by day or night service. Tours are operated by a number of companies of which possibly the best known is Scottish Omnibuses Ltd, New Street, Edinburgh, and 302 Buchanan Street, Glasgow. Apart from a large number of day tours, this company offers excellent extended tours from Edinburgh and Glasgow, using comfortable coaches and the best accommodation available in the areas selected. Tours available from 3 to 10 days duration cover the most scenic parts of the country.

Tour schedules run from the end of April to mid-September.

A network of long distance buses, local buses and rural postbuses covers Scotland. Timetables are available from the Scottish Tourist Board (address on p. 35) and the many local information services throughout the country (see pp. 36–42).

Europabus, a coach service operated by the railways of western Europe, also provides swift, comfortable travel to Scotland from London which includes tours of the Highlands. Because of the frequent changes in prices, it is advisable to get details from British Rail Travel Centres (see p. 34).

IF YOU ARE MOTORING

Car Sleepers The use of these services can save an immense amount of tedious driving on the over-crowded roads of England and central Scotland. Currently, there are motorail services from London to Edinburgh, Aberdeen, Perth and Stirling; from Southampton, Bristol, Newton Abbot, Inverness and Dover to Stirling; from Newcastle, York and Crewe to Inverness; from Crewe to Perth and Inverness; and from Cambridge to Edinburgh.

Car Ferries The following table summarizes the main services, both to the islands and on the mainland. Some of the services do not operate on Sunday. Advance booking is usually essential on services to the islands. Full details from the motoring organizations (addresses on pp. 34, 35).

Most, but not all, are drive-on ferries.

Island	Port of Departure	Port of Arrival
Arran	Ardrossan	Brodick
	Claonaig (Kintyre)	Lochranza
Barra	Oban	Castlebay
Bute	Wemyss Bay	Rothesay
	Colintraive	Rhubodach
Colonsay, Coll, Tiree	Oban	Colonsay, Coll, Tiree
Cumbrae	Largs	Cumbrae slip for Millport
Harris	Uig (Skye)	Tarbert
Islay	Kennacraig	Port Askaig
	West Loch Tarbert	Port Ellen
Jura	Port Askaig (Islay)	Feolin
Lewis	Ullapool	Stornoway
Mull	Oban	Craignure
	Lochaline	Fishnish
North Uist	Uig (Skye)	Lochmaddy
	Tarbert (Harris)	Lochmaddy
Orkney	Aberdeen	Kirkwall
	Scrabster	Stromness
Seil and Luing	Cuan (Seil)	Luing
Shetland	Aberdeen	Lerwick
Skye	Mallaig	Armadale
	Kyle of Lochalsh	Kyleakin
South Uist	Oban	Lochboisdale

Mainland

Corran/Ardgour	Weekdays 08.15 (Sundays 10.00) to 20.45 (June to August).
Gourock/Dunoon	Weekdays 06.45 to 22.00; Sundays 08.45 to 20.00.
Invergordon	Across the Cromarty Firth to Balblair. May to September infrequently between 09.40 and 17.40.
Kessock	Links Black Isle to Inverness across the Beauly Firth. Weekdays 07.30 to 22.30; Sundays 10.00 to 18.00.
Kylesku	Across Loch Cairnbawn. Daily 09.00 to dusk.

Car Rental It is advisable to rent a car in advance, although the international firms have several agencies in Scotland. Rates vary enormously according to season and the type of car rented. The Scottish Tourist Board (address on p. 35) has a leaflet *Car Hire in Scotland* which gives details throughout the country.

ACCOMMODATION

Hotels Hotels of every class are listed in a national register of accommodation published by the Scottish Tourist Board (address on p. 35)—
Where to Stay in Scotland. This lists hotels, boarding houses and bed

and breakfast accommodation, all over the country, and another publication called *Self Catering Accommodation in Scotland* lists houses, cottages and caravans to let. These guides are for sale from the Scottish Tourist Board.

Local tourist offices (look for the sign 'i') operate a scheme called Book-a-bed-ahead. The visitor pays a small deposit per head (which is deducted from the hotel or boarding house bill at the end of his stay) plus an additional small charge for the telephone or telex call, and for this the tourist office books the required accommodation. The scheme is fairly new and is working very well, and is especially useful to visitors in the busy season.

If you should find yourself in need of bed and breakfast accommodation in a remote area, enquire at the local post office. Quite often the postmaster will be able to recommend someone, although, of course, this is not part of his official duties.

Youth Hostels The Scottish Youth Hostels Association provides cheap overnight accommodation of a simple type in many parts of the country. Membership fees are low and benefits high.

Visitors from abroad may become International Members but it is always cheaper for the visitor to join his own country's hostelling association before leaving home.

Overnight charges vary according to the grade of the hostel. Members must bring, or hire, a sheet sleeping bag. Meals are available at some hostels, but all have cooking facilities where members may cook their own food. Young people from all over the world use the Scottish hostels, and prior booking is advisable. The Association's handbook lists all hostels, and the choice is extremely varied. Garth, at Fortingall, was once a gracious country house while Carbisdale at Culrain is a most imposing castle, once the home of the Duchess of Sutherland.

The SYHA also offers sports holidays to members—sailing and canoeing on Loch Lomond, or pony trekking in various parts of the country.

Although the hostels are primarily intended for walkers and cyclists, those using a car may stay provided there is sufficient room.

The addresses of the Edinburgh, Glasgow and Aberdeen Youth Hostels are: 7 Bruntsfield Crescent, Edinburgh EH10 4EZ, and 17/18 Eglinton Crescent, Edinburgh EH12 5DD; 10 Woodlands Terrace, Glasgow G3 6DD; King George VI Memorial Hostel, 8 Queens Road, Aberdeen AB1 6Y2. Further information may be obtained from the SYHA, 7 Glebe Crescent, Stirling FK8 2JA.

Camping and Caravanning All over Scotland there are beautiful places for pitching a tent. The farmer or crofter concerned will usually give permission, provided the campers undertake to do no damage and leave no litter. There are also organized sites where basic facilities are available. These are listed in the Scottish Tourist Board's gazetteer of camping and caravan (trailer) sites and facilities, called *Scotland for Touring Caravans*, covering both the mainland and the Outer Isles. Their *Self Catering Accommodation in Scotland* lists static sites where caravans can be hired.

EATING

In all the main centres there is the usual rash of Indian, Chinese, Italian restaurants, although not all are licensed. These are usually open until 11 p.m. or midnight. Of all the Scottish cities Edinburgh is richest in good restaurants. Booking is almost always necessary. In remoter parts, however, it may be difficult to get a meal after 8 p.m.

Visitors who would like to try specifically Scottish food should look out for the following traditional dishes: **haggis**—a mixture of offal finely chopped, highly seasoned, mixed with oatmeal and onions, and sewn into a bag traditionally made from the lining of a sheep's stomach; **porridge**—made by adding oatmeal to boiling salted water and eaten usually at breakfast, with thin cream or milk; **Scotch broth**—a thick vegetable soup; **cock-a-leekie**—soup made from chicken and leeks; **smoked fish**—kippers, Arbroath smokies, Finnan haddies, and, of course, smoked salmon; **oatcakes**—savoury biscuits made from oatmeal; **shortbread**—pale, thick biscuit made from flour, butter and sugar; **black bun**—spicy fruit cake encased in thin flat pastry. They are not necessarily available everywhere, though there is a move to encourage hotels and restaurants, under the Taste of Scotland scheme, to serve more Scottish fare.

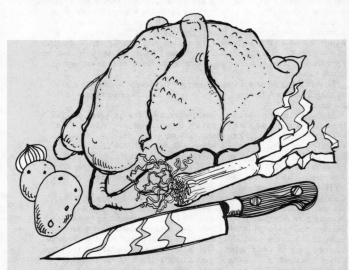

FESTIVALS AND EVENTS

January	Burning of the Clavie at Burghead (13 km/8 ml N of Elgin)—a revival of a Norse and Celtic fire festival celebrated on 11 January. A tar barrel is set alight, carried to the top of Dourie Hill and rolled down
	Burns Suppers—held all over Scotland to commemorate the birth on 25 January of Scotland's national poet Robert Burns (1759). Haggis is eaten with turnip and potatoes, the drink is whisky and the speeches follow a set traditional pattern and include the recital of some of Burns' poems
	Lerwick, Shetland—Up Helly Aa, the most spectacular of the fire festivals, held on the last Tuesday in January, re-enacts the Norse invasions with costumed Vikings and a Viking galley which is set ablaze by hundreds of flaming torches
	Stonehaven—one of the ancient Norse and Celtic fire festivals when fire balls are swung around the head on 1 January
February	Cairngorm—Scottish Skiing Championships
March	Aviemore—curling events
April	Dunfermline—Carnegie Festival of music and arts
	Pitlochry—theatre season from end of April to beginning of October
May	Arran—Spring Weekend, usually mid-month
	Ballater—Royal Deeside golf week
	Drymen—agricultural show
	Loch Leven—angling championships
	Nairn—golf week
	Perth—festival of the arts, usually from mid to end May

Skye Week—when the chieftain calls the clansmen back to the island of their forebears, usually held at the end of May

Stirling—festival of music, drama and the arts for two weeks

Stranraer—pipe band contests, varies from end of May to early June

Trossachs—water sports festival, varies from May to June

Wester Ross—Countryside Festival (films, talks, cruises and ceilidhs) held all over the area for two weeks

June

Borders—Common Riding events which are special ceremonies held on varying dates in Hawick, Selkirk, Peebles, Galashiels, also in Lanark, Dumfries and Dunfermline. A Common Riding is traditionally when an appointed citizen leads others on horseback around the boundaries of the town. Streets are decorated, and there are events for children.

Edinburgh—Royal Highland Show (an agricultural show designed to appeal to the townsman as well as the farmer) usually held the third week in June

Lairg—sheep dog trials

Stirling—agricultural show

July

Agricultural Shows—at Kelso, Skye and Haddington

Anstruther—seafood festival

Borders—Common Riding and other similar festivities in Duns, Kelso, Annan, Castle Douglas, Jedburgh, St Boswells, Kelso and Langholm.

Highland Games—at Inveraray, Rothesay, Durness, Tobermory, Luss, Gourock, Lochearnhead and Arisaig. Check dates locally

Inverness—Combined Services Tattoo from last Thursday in July to first Wednesday in August

Islay—sheep dog trials—third week

	Stirling—on the Saturday nearest Midsummer Day there is always a procession headed by bagpipes and banners from Stirling to the battlefield where Bannockburn was fought in 1314
August	Aberdeen—International Festival of Youth Orchestras
	Agricultural Shows—at Perth, Turriff, Keith, Lamlash, Biggar, Peebles, Dumfries and Kirkwall
	Edinburgh International Festival of Music and Drama—end of August to early September for three weeks
	Hawick—World Pipe Band championships
	Highland Gatherings—at Strathpeffer, Ayr, Brodick, Nairn, Dornoch, Inverness, Newtonmore, Portree, Dunoon, Oban, Fort William, Bute and Ballater. Check dates locally
	Kirkcudbright—Summer School in arts and crafts
	Stonehaven—annual regatta
	West Highland Yachting Week—Crinan/Oban/Tobermory
September	Ben Navis Race—first week
	Highland Gatherings—at Aboyne, Braemar, Pitlochry, Shotts
	Mull Week
	Newcastleton—Liddesdale agricultural show
	Oban—Whisky festival
October	Arran—Autumn Weekend, usually at the end of the month
	Cattle shows—at Oban and Perth
	The Mod—its venue changes but this above all is the most exclusively Scottish event in the calendar—a competitive meeting for singers, soloists, choirs and instrumentalists. It is conducted in Gaelic and is widely publicized and followed, even by those who don't speak the language

The Scottish Tourist Board (address on p. 35) publishes *Scotland: 600 Things to See,* which will keep you well-informed. Anyone who wants an active holiday should collect all the information possible before he maps out his time. Scotland offers such a wealth of outdoor and sporting facilities that you could easily miss the chance of a lifetime to see, say, the wild geese in their thousands fly over the Solway, or to spend a few days learning something completely new to you like water skiing or canoeing. Here are a few of the possibilities:

Agricultural shows These are usually held in midsummer and are advertised locally. Your local tourist office should be able to tell you the dates of shows in the area. There is no better way of seeing the rural population of Scotland enjoying itself. Usually these shows comprise livestock competitions, baking, crafts and flower arranging competitions, Highland dancing competitions, show jumping competitions and usually a great deal of selling by suppliers to the farming community who take stalls around the showground. The largest event of this kind is the Royal Highland Show (held in June), at its permanent site at Ingliston, outside Edinburgh, and since it is expensive to organize, it normally includes a lot of extra attractions to bring in the townspeople. Agricultural shows in rural areas have a more intimate and friendly flavour.

Crafts There are craft workshops in Arran, at Balnakeil in N Sutherland and, increasingly, they are springing up around the country. If you are particularly interested in any one craft—say, handloom weaving, potting or wrought iron work—it may be worth writing to the Scottish Tourist Board and also to the Small Industries Council (addresses on p. 35) as they both produce booklets about craftsmen who like to be visited. They cover every imaginable craft and all parts of the country. If you use this information to help plan a car tour, it will give you unrivalled opportunities of buying good quality and authentic souvenirs of the country.

Highland Gatherings These are held all over Scotland from early summer to autumn and are an absolute feast for the photographer. The usual ingredients are Highland dancing competitions, piping competitions and, for the strong men, trials like putting the shot, throwing the hammer and tossing the caber. The showground will be awash with tartan and if you have a portable tape recorder you can take home some of the authentic sounds of Scotland. Dates vary so your best source of information is the local tourist office.

Horse racing Among the places where race meetings take place regularly are Ayr, Hamilton, Lanark and Musselburgh.

Loch Ness Monster Drive from Inverness towards Castle Urquhart on the shores of Loch Ness. If it is a still, sunny day you may be lucky! While a great deal of effort has as yet failed to prove that the

monster *does* exist, it certainly has not been proved that it does *not* exist. We have not only hundreds of contemporary eye-witness accounts, but St Adamnan, writing about St Columba in the 6th century, tells how he quelled the monster when it threatened a swimmer. The local people around Loch Ness have always known of its presence, but the greater public did not hear of it until the 1930s when newspaper publicity made it famous.

Many theories have been advanced as to what the monster actually is. To me, the most convincing one is that it is a type of plesiosaurus which was trapped when Loch Ness became separated from the sea about 10,000 years ago. I incline to this theory because the plesiosaurus *looks* right, but whether this is the original monster or a descendant, and what it lives on, are questions the scientists are still arguing about.

Motor racing There is a road racing circuit at Ingliston, on the outskirts of Edinburgh, where meetings are held from April to October.

Nature Few countries in Europe have so much wild open country where nature can be seen in all its unspoiled glory. You can see animals that are, or were, indigenous to Scotland—wolves, reindeer, wildcat and perhaps an eagle at the Highland Wildlife Park, Kincraig, Kingussie. There is a drive through part of this 80-hectare (200-acre) estate, which also includes a cafe and picnic area and a walking area. It is on the Perth/Inverness road A9 between Aviemore and Kingussie. For more exotic animals try Cameron House, Loch Lomond (bison and yak) and the Safari Park, Doune. But if you want nature stark and unspoiled make for Glenmore Forest Park, and go first to the Carrbridge visitors' centre to get the layout of the area. There are wonderful things to be seen—osprey, the crested tit, or even capercailzie if you are lucky (its camouflage is incredibly good).

Hides are provided at two places from which to observe ospreys— Loch Garten in Speyside, and Loch of the Lowes, near Dunkeld.

Golden eagles are most likely to be seen flying overhead in the Cuillin area of Skye.

There are, in Scotland, a vast number of nature trails (mainly run by the Nature Conservancy) and forest walks (Forestry Commission). Most of them have a picnic area and some kind of information kiosk. You can write in advance for details to the Nature Conservancy and Forestry Commission (addresses on p. 35), the Scottish Tourist Board has free information, and details are also available locally at tourist information offices who are always pleased to tell you what to see in their area.

Sheep Dog Trials These are a special feature of the Borders, and the obedience and discipline of the sheepdogs are most impressive. The Scottish Tourist Board will supply a list of dates and places for the coming season free of charge.

Theatre Serious drama, as opposed to seaside revue, can be seen principally in Edinburgh, Glasgow, Aberdeen, Dundee, Perth, St Andrews, Dervaig on Mull, Ochtertyre near Crieff, Inverness, Pitlochry, and the MacRobert Centre on the Stirling University campus. There is a great deal of musical activity in Scotland too, and enquiries should be made locally at the tourist information offices.

Whisky Glenfiddich Distillery, south of Elgin, has a visitors' centre where the public are most welcome. Around the Inverness area, the names of local distilleries sound like a roll-call from a well-stocked bar. Locally the visiting of distilleries is called 'going on the whisky trail'. The local tourist office can give you a list of places where visitors are welcome.

Stately Homes Scotland has so many stately homes that it would be impossible to include the list here. You can't move around Scotland without being reminded of its history. Make sure you don't miss a particularly lovely mansion, dramatic castle, abbey, or special set of treasures by getting all the relevant information from the Scottish Tourist Board and a list of the National Trust's properties in Scotland (addresses on p. 35).

Gardens Himalayan plants have always done well in this country so rhododendron, azaleas and meconopsis are always grown in abundance. In spring the daffodils are magnificent—they seem to scent the very air of the Borders—as are the wild iris in the Highlands and islands. In autumn there is the opportunity to see the indigenous plants of Scotland at their blazing best—the combination on a hillside of rowan trees, golden bracken and purple heather will delight all plantsmen.

Robert Burns, Mary Queen of Scots, Sir Walter Scott If you have always been interested in any of these notable Scots, why not plan a tour round Scotland in their footsteps. The Scottish Tourist Board has excellent leaflets which tell you how to trace Robert Burns' life around the country—the places he lived in, and wrote in—and provides the same information on Scott, pointing out the actual sites he described in his works. Queen Mary's story is a sad one and a tour based on the places of importance to her will give the visitor a good idea of what Scotland was like in the 16th century.

Birdwatching There is so much birdlife around the country, apart from organized Nature Reserves, that you should collect as much information as possible before your holiday on what particularly interests you. The Royal Society for the Protection of Birds, the Scottish Field Studies Association, Nature Conservancy and the Scottish Wildlife Trust (addresses on p. 35) may be able to advise you on your particular interests.

Cruising You are bound to enjoy a few hours afloat—especially if you do your cruising on a ferry, big or small, with nothing more strenuous to do than admire the scenery. Pride of place goes to the *Waverley* which plies up and down the Clyde, and is the last sea-going paddle steamer in the world. But the *Maid of the Loch* which cruises on Loch Lomond, is also highly popular. With a coastline like ours, especially in the west, there are many ferries plying between the narrowest points.

Black-throated diver

If you go over on the tiny ferry from Bunessan on Mull to Iona, there will hardly be time to enjoy the scenery but it will certainly put some clear fresh air into your lungs and a glow of colour on your face. There are several ferries like this around the coast.

The big Hebridean ferries of Caledonian MacBrayne Ltd run from Mallaig and Oban and serve all the islands. You can map out an adventurous holiday programme and see some magnificent scenery and out of the ordinary places by making these boats your mode of holiday transport. Pleasure cruises can be taken from such west-coast resorts as Ardrossan, Dunoon, Oban, Largs, Rothesay, Brodick and Millport.

Fishing Fishing in a strange country is fraught with problems—what kind of fish can one hope for, how much will it cost, how does one get a permit, who owns the fishing rights, when is the close season? The Scottish Tourist Board has done all the spadework for enthusiasts by publishing two booklets *Scotland for Fishing* and *Scotland for Sea Angling*. They answer every possible question, and the visitor can do no better than buy these inexpensive booklets.

Golf Everybody associates golf with Scotland and the names of famous courses of this country make sweet music for any enthusiast—St Andrews, Turnberry, Gleneagles, Old Prestwick, Carnoustie, Muirfield. Each course has its own personality, its own hazards, its own perfect views. If you intend playing golf when you come to Scotland, good practical advice about where and when and how much is given in the Scottish Tourist Board's booklet *Scotland Home of Golf* which lists over 300 courses where visitors may play, and each entry has very helpful notes about the relevant rules and restrictions.

Hillwalking Scotland is a country offering great opportunity for hillwalking but knowing where, when and how to go can pose problems for the visitor. Walks are not always as well signposted as in some European countries—everything in Scotland is much wilder, grander and less organized. Local information is always available at hotels and tourist information offices but the Scottish Tourist Board has an excellent booklet called *Scotland for Hillwalking* which details over 50 walks throughout the country. Most Scottish hills can be climbed in one day but, though not high by Alpine standards, they can be distinctly dangerous, and no one should venture on to the hills without the proper footwear and clothing.

Riding One tends to think of pony trekking, because of its great rise in popularity, but, though there is ample opportunity to pursue that sport, Scotland also offers good hard riding country for more experienced horsemen. If horses are your passion you should look primarily to the Borders area—Melrose and Jedburgh are centres for trail riding. Pony trekking is available at—amongst other places— Peebles, Yetholm, Dunbar, Gifford, Aviemore, Kingussie, Newtonmore, Trossachs, Arran, Mull and Skye. The Scottish Tourist Board will be able to provide details of all-in holidays or to supply information on where to hire a mount for a day's excursion.

Sailing If you have ever wondered about the fascination of messing about in boats, here is your chance to find out. Scotland is a good place to learn—there are schools on the west coast and schools on inland lochs. The Scottish Tourist Board will give you details of sailing opportunities, or write to the Scottish Sports Council (address on p. 35). If you are already experienced, of course, you may prefer to bring your own boat, or to join as crew on a cruise.

Swimming There are still many empty beaches in Scotland but unless it is a scorching summer you may well find that the water temperature and coastal winds take much of the pleasure out of a dip. For this reason many small resorts have pool facilities.

Water Skiing With so many lochs it is not surprising that water skiing has become popular in Scotland. You may be unlikely to do it in a bikini, since we can hardly claim to have a Mediterranean climate, but local clubs and skiing schools will keep you right about gear.
Sub aqua facilities are available at two centres, Oban and Coldingham.

Winter Sports Scotland may now be regarded as a skiing country, although the sport is relatively new and not so highly mechanized as it is elsewhere in Europe. There are slopes in the Cairngorms, Glenshee and Upper Deeside and Glencoe. The Cairngorm area includes the little towns of Newtonmore, Kingussie, Kincraig, Aviemore, Boat of Garten, Carrbridge, Grantown on Spey and Nethybridge, and accommodation is being steadily increased.

At Cairngorm an access road leads to the car park at 610 m (2000 ft) and chains or snow tyres are sometimes necessary. Chairlifts and T-bar tows operate on Coire Cas and Coir na Ciste. The White Lady Sheiling shelter and restaurant is adjacent to the car park, and at the top of the chairlift is the highest restaurant in Britain, the Ptarmigan at 1189 m (3900 ft).

At Glenshee and Upper Deeside there are runs on the Cairnwell mountain and Meall Odhar. Ballater, Braemar, Blairgowrie, Pitlochry and Glenshee are the main accommodation centres for this area. There is a chairlift at 670 m (2200 ft) on Cairnwell with a cafe at the terminal, and a 500-m (550-yd) ski tow on the opposite side of the Braemar–Perth road.

At Glencoe the car park is on the moor below Meall a Bhuiridh. Chairlifts and tows lead to the top of the mountain. Hot drinks are on sale at a mountain chalet, and there are some hotels nearby.

Full details of the ski schools and hotels operating in these districts are set out in *Winter Sports in Scotland,* available from the Scottish Sports Council or the Scottish Tourist Board (addresses on p. 35).

Although the season may well extend into May, conditions are by no means Alpine, and you should be prepared for dull conditions, cold winds and a lot of ice. Equipment may be rented at all centres, but you should invest in a pair of boots, as an ill-fitting pair can make life a misery. Instruction is available at all centres.

The National Trust for Scotland exists to protect and to care for fine buildings and beautiful scenery. It has in its care an extremely wide variety of properties—castles and country houses, historic sites, water falls, dovecotes, gardens, mountain areas, little houses and properties associated with famous Scots. In Ayrshire there is **Culzean Castle** and its gardens. This castle was designed by Robert Adam for the 10th Earl of Cassillis in the 18th century. It is a most beautiful building to visit, and the public can explore the 200 hectares (500 acres) of gardens, woodland and shore which comprise Culzean Country Park. The home farm building has been converted into a reception centre and visitor complex. Meals are served in the restaurant there.

A different kind of property is the Royal Burgh of **Culross** in Fife. A wholly delightful little town, this is a beautiful example of Scottish domestic architecture of the 16th and 17th centuries. For many years the National Trust, in collaboration with local authorities and other bodies, has been restoring the buildings—from small flats, now modernized and let to tenants, to the mansion known as the Palace. This is now maintained by the Department of the Environment. At The Study, visitors can get guidance on how best to tour the little town from the Trust's representative.

The Trust also owns large stretches of land. One of its most popular properties is **Inverewe Gardens** at Poolewe, Wester Ross. This part of the coast is warmed by the Gulf Stream and a belt of trees planted by the original owner has made it possible for this sheltered garden to become the home of exotic tropical plants and botanical rarities. Spring is the best time to visit Inverewe, but it is open all year. There is a licensed restaurant in operation during the summer.

Membership of the Trust costs only a few pounds a year. Admission to its properties is free to members. The Trust owns about 80 properties around the country so if you would like to visit a few of these places while touring Scotland, an annual subscription represents quite a saving—it doesn't take long to run through the subscription in individual admission charges to even a few properties. Membership details available from The National Trust for Scotland (address on p. 35), which will also supply a list of its properties.

Crathes Castle (above)   *Pittenweem, Fife (below)*

SHOPPING

Edinburgh and Glasgow are undoubtedly the best shopping centres simply because they are the largest, and can therefore offer the widest variety. Many visitors have heard that Scotland is a good centre for **antiques**, which is certainly true. Edinburgh seems to be full of antique shops, but the enthusiast should also make for Perth, Glasgow, Aberdeen, Crieff and up as far as Thurso. Almost every small town will have an antique dealer of some kind, and if his shop is not obvious it is as well to enquire (the local furniture shop or jeweller can usually tell you who deals in second hand goods).

For **woollen goods,** Inverness and the Borders are good centres after the big cities. There are also good shops in both Oban and Fort William where mohair rugs and coats, as well as the ubiquitous cashmere sweaters are worth looking at. In recent years there has been a proliferation of woollen mill shops. The goods there, though rarely of high fashion, are frequently good value for money.

Silver **jewellery** from Shetland is beautifully designed but you do not have to go to the source for it; jewellers around the mainland have been quick to appreciate its clean uncluttered lines.

Glass of all kinds makes an attractive gift. Paperweights made in both Caithness and Crieff are well known to collectors of such articles.

Some of the more unusual **souvenirs** you might like to buy are rugs made from the hide of red deer, Shetland sweaters knitted specially for you (enquire at Highland Home Industries, George Street, Edinburgh), spoons, egg cups and napkin rings made from deer horn, Edinburgh crystal wine glasses in the shape of a thistle, table mats in black or red with the Celtic 'eternal' design scrolled in gold—all of these and many more are real mementoes of the craftsmanship of Scotland.

USEFUL ADDRESSES

American Consulate, 3 Regent Street, Edinburgh (Tel. 031-556-2061)

Automobile Association, Fanum House, Erskine Harbour, Erskine, Renfrewshire (Tel. 041-812-0144)

British Airways, 122 St Vincent Street, Glasgow G2 (Tel. 041-332-9666)

British Caledonian Airways, 127 Buchanan Street, Glasgow G1 (Tel. 041-332-1681)

British Rail Travel Centre, 4 Lower Regent Street, London SW1 (Tel. 01-930-4792) or any railway station enquiries desk

Caledonian MacBrayne Ltd, The Pier, Gourock, Renfrewshire (Tel. Gourock 33755)

City of Edinburgh Tourist Information and Accommodation Service, 1 Cockburn Street, Edinburgh EH1 1BP (Tel. 031-226-6591)

City of Glasgow Information Bureau, George Square, Glasgow G2 1ES (Tel. 041-221-9600)

Corporation of the City of Aberdeen, St Nicholas House, Broad Street, Aberdeen (Tel. Aberdeen 23456)

Corporation of Dundee, City Square, Dundee (Tel. Dundee 23141)
Department of the Environment (who control many of Scotland's
   Ancient Monuments), Argyle House, 3 Lady Lawson Street,
   Edinburgh EH3 9DR (Tel. 031-229-9191); Area office (West), 187 George
   Street, Glasgow G1 (Tel. 041-552-4455)
Forestry Commission, 231 Corstrophine Road, Edinburgh 12 (Tel.
   031-334-0303); Portcullis House, India Street, Glasgow G2 (Tel.
   041-248-3931)
Golden Rail, PO Box 12, York YO1 1YX
Highland and Islands Development Board, PO Box 7, Inverness.
Loganair Ltd, St Andrew's Drive, Glasgow Airport, Paisley PA3 2TG
   (Tel. 041-889-3181)
National Trust for Scotland, 5 Charlotte Square, Edinburgh EH2 4DU
   (Tel. 031-226-5922); 7 West George Street, Glasgow G2 (Tel. 041-248-
   3294)
Nature Conservancy, 12 Hope Terrace, Edinburgh EH9 2AS (Tel.
   031-447-4784); Regional HQ for SW Scotland, The Castle, Loch
   Lomond Park, Balloch (Tel. Alexandria 53511)
North of Scotland, Orkney and Shetland Shipping Co, Matthew's Quay,
   Aberdeen (Tel. Aberdeen 29111)
Royal Automobile Club, 17 Rutland Square, Edinburgh (Tel. 031-229-
   3555); 242 West George Street, Glasgow G2 (Tel. 041-248-4444)
Royal Society for the Protection of Birds, 17 Regent Terrace, Edinburgh
   EH7 5BN (Tel. 031-556-5624)
Scotland's Gardens Scheme (details of gardens open to the public),
   26 Castle Terrace, Edinburgh EH1 2EL (Tel. 031-229-1870)
Scottish Field Studies Association, Forelands, 18 Market Gate, Crail,
   Fife KY10 3TL
Scottish Sports Council, 1 St Colme Street, Edinburgh (Tel. 031-225-5544);
   16 Royal Crescent, Glasgow G3 (Tel. 041-332-9416)
Scottish Tourist Board: call for information at 2 Rutland Place,
   Edinburgh (Tel. 031-332-2433); correspondence only to 23 Ravelston
   Terrace, Edinburgh EH4 3EU
Scottish Wildlife Trust, 8 Dublin Street, Edinburgh EH1 3PP (Tel.
   031-556-4199)
Scottish Youth Hostels Association, 7 Glebe Crescent, Stirling FK8
   2JA (Tel. Stirling 2821)
Small Industries Council, 27 Walker Street, Edinburgh 3 (Tel. 031-225-
   2846)
Western Ferries, Kennacraig, West Loch Tarbert, Argyll (Tel.
   Whitehouse (Argyll) 218)

Tourist Information Centres

These centres will help you with accommodation. They will also prove
very helpful in telling you about local places worth a visit, and about
the various events taking place in their area. Centres displaying a
'bed' sign will book accommodation in advance. The 'C' printed in
some of the entries below indicates the centre to which all postal
enquiries should be sent. NTS is National Trust for Scotland.

THE BORDERS

All correspondence to Borders
Tourist Association,
66 Woodmarket, Kelso,
Roxburghshire

Berwick-upon-Tweed
Castlegate Car Park, Tel: 7187
mid May–mid Oct

Coldstream
High Street, Tel: 2486
Apr–mid Sep

Ettrick Valley
Post Office, Tel: 221

Galashiels
Reiver Gallery
Gala Park Road, Tel: 4208

Grantshouse
Border Reivers Craft Shop
Easter–Oct

Hawick
Volunteer Park, Tel: 2547
mid May–mid Oct

Jedburgh
Lothian Park, Tel: 3435
mid May–mid Oct

Kelso
66 Woodmarket, Tel: 2125

Lauder
9 Mid Row, Tel: 389

Peebles
High Street, Tel: 21038
mid May–mid Oct

Selkirk
Luckenbooth, Market Place,
Tel: 3709

SOUTH WEST

All correspondence to
South West Scotland
Tourist Association,
Douglas House, Newton
Stewart, Wigtownshire

Castle Douglas
Markethill, Tel: 2611
May–Sep

**Culzean Castle
(NTS)**
Tel: Kirkoswald 274. Mar–Oct

Dalbeattie
52 High Street, Tel: 259

Dumfries
Whitesands, Tel: 3862
May–Sep

Gatehouse-of-Fleet
Horatio Square, Tel: 212
May–Sep

Girvan
Bridge Street, Tel: 2056

Kirkcudbright
Harbour Square, Tel: 30494
May–Sep

Lochmaben
Town Hall, Tel: 265

Lockerbie
55 High Street, Tel: 2123

New Cumnock
Town Hall, Tel: 581
Jun–Sep

Newton Stewart
Dashwood Square, Tel: 2431
May–Sep

Stranraer
Church Street, Tel: 2601
Breastwork Car Park, Tel: 2595
mid May–Sep

EDINBURGH AND LOTHIANS

All correspondence to
The Edinburgh & Lothians
Tourist Association, 1 Cockburn
Street, Edinburgh EH1 1BP

Edinburgh
1 Cockburn Street, Tel:
031-226-6591
Scottish Tourist Board,
2 Rutland Place
Tel: 031-332-2433

Dunbar
Town House, High Street
Tel: 3353

North Berwick
Quality Street, Tel: 2197
mid Nov–Sep

GLASGOW AND CLYDE

All correspondence to
The Clyde Tourist Assocation,
Information Bureau, George
Square, Glasgow G2 1ES

Abington
'Little Chef', Tel: 636

Jun–Sep
Airdrie
Municipal Buildings,
Tel: 62453
Ayr
30 Miller Road, Tel: 68077
Balloch
Tel: Alexandria 53533
Jun–Sep
Biggar
Main Street, Tel: 20259
Jun–Sep
Brodick, Isle of Arran
The Pier, Tel: 2401
Glasgow
George Square, Tel: 041-221-9600
or 041-221-7371
Gourock
Pierhead, Tel: 31126
Greenock
Municipal Buildings, Clyde
Square, Tel: 24400
Helensburgh
Pier Car Park, Tel: 0436
Jun–Sep
Lamlash, Isle of Arran
County Offices, Tel: 385
Largs
The Pier, Tel: 3765
Millport, Isle of Cumbrae
Garrison House, Tel: 356
Old Pier, Tel: 314
Nov–Sep
Prestwick
Station Road, Tel: 77084
Prestwick Airport, Tel: 77309
Rothesay, Isle of Bute
West Pier, Tel: 2151
Tarbet
Stuckgowan, Tel: Arrochar 251
Jun–Sep
Troon
14 Templehill, Tel: 314455

TAYSIDE

All correspondence to
Perthshire and Central
Highlands Tourist Association,
Marshall Place, Perth
PH2 8NS

Aberfeldy
The Square, Tel: 276
mid May–mid Sep
Blairgowrie
Wellmeadow, Tel: 2960
mid May–Sep
Crieff
James Square, Tel: 2578
end Mar–early Oct
Dunkeld (NTS)
The Square, Tel: 460
Easter–Oct
Glenshee
Wellmeadow, Blairgowrie,
Tel: Blairgowrie 2960
May–Sep
11 Panmure Street, Dundee,
Tel: Dundee 23688
Killiecrankie (NTS)
Tel: 233. Easter–mid Oct
Kenmore
Library Building, Tel: 295
mid Jun–Sep
Perth
Marshall Place, PH2 8NS
Tel: 22900/27108
Pitlochry
28 Atholl Road, Tel: 2215
All correspondence direct to
the following:
Arbroath
105 High Street, Tel: 2609
Carnoustie
24 High Street, Tel: 52258
The Links, Tel: 52258
Jun–Sep
Dundee
City Square, Tel: 23141
Monifieth
Municipal Chambers,
High Street, Tel: 2152
Montrose
212 High Street, Tel: 2000

FIFE

All correspondence to Fife
Tourist Association, High
Street, Leven KY8 4OA
Burntisland
Publicity Officer, 4 Kirkgate

Dunfermline
Glenbridge Car Park. May–Sep
Falkland Palace (NTS)
Tel: Falkland 397
end Mar–mid Oct
Glenrothes
Town Centre, Tel: 4954
Kirkcaldy
Esplanade, May–Sep
Leven
Fife Tourist Association,
High Street, Tel: 3327
South Street, Tel: 2533
Newport-on-Tay
Forgan Roundabout,
Tel: Newport 3034
May–Sep
St Andrews
South Street, Tel: 2021

CENTRAL

All correspondence to Central
Scotland Tourist Association,
Woodlands, St Ninians Road,
Stirling FK8 2HB
Aberfoyle
Main Street, Tel: 352
Apr–Oct
David Marshall Lodge,
Tel: 258. Mid Mar–mid Oct
Bannockburn Monument (NTS)
Tel: Bannockburn 2664
Apr–mid Oct
Ben Lawers (NTS)
Tel: Killin 397
May–Sep
Callander
Leny Road, Tel: 30342
Apr–Oct
Killin
Main Street, Tel: 254
May–Sep
Lix Toll Garage, Tel: 280
Lochearnhead
Tel: 220. Apr–Oct
Stirling
Dumbarton Road, Tel: 5019
Apr–Oct
Tyndrum
Post Office, Tel: 246. Apr–Oct

GRAMPIAN

Correspondence excluding
Aberdeen to: Grampian Tourist
Association, 17 High Street,
Elgin, Moray IV30 1EG;
for Aberdeen, to Publicity
Dept., St. Nicholas House,
Broad Street, Aberdeen,
Tel: 23456/24890
Aberdeen
Stonehaven Road, Tel: 50060
mid May–mid Sep
Sea Beach, Tel: 50000
mid Jun–mid Sep
Ballater
Station Square, Tel: 306
May–Oct
Banchory
Dee Street Car Park, Tel: 2000
May–Oct
Banff
Collie Lodge, Tel: 2419
Jun–Sep
Braemar
Fife Arms Mews, Tel: 600
May–Oct
Cullen
20 Seafield Street, Tel: 757
Jun–Sep
Dufftown
The Square, Tel: 501
Jun–Sep
Elgin
High Street, Tel: 3388
May–Oct
Ellon
The Square, Tel: 730
Jun–Sep
Fochabers
Public Institute, High Street,
Tel: 555. Jun–Sep
Forres
Town Hall, High Street,
Tel: 2278. Jun–Sep

Traquair House

The Square, Kelso

Fraserburgh
Saltoun Square, Tel: 2315
Jun–Sep
Huntly
The Square, Tel: 2255
Jun–Sep
Inverurie
The Square, Tel: 2600
Jun–Sep
Keith
Church Street, Tel: 2634
Jun–Sep
Stonehaven
The Square, Tel: 2806
May–Oct
Tomintoul
Main Street, Tel: 285
May–Oct

HIGHLANDS AND ISLANDS

Ardgartan
Tel: Arrochar 388. Apr–Sep
C: Dunoon
Aviemore
Aviemore Centre Car Park,
Tel: 363
Balmacara (NTS)
Lochalsh House, Kyle of
Lochalsh, Tel: 207
Jun–Sep
Bonar Bridge
Tel: Ardgay 333. Mid May–Sep
C: Dornoch
Bowmore, Isle of Islay
Tel: 254. Apr–Sep
C: Campbeltown
Broadford, Isle of Skye
Tel: 361. May–Oct
C: Portree
Brora
Tel: 465. Mid May–Sep
C: Dornoch
Campbeltown
Tel: 2056
Carrbridge
High Street, Tel: 630
May–Sep
Castlebay, Isle of Barra
Tel: 336. May–Sep
C: Stornoway

Culloden Battlefield (NTS)
Culloden Moor, Tel: Culloden
Moor 607. Apr–mid Oct
Dornoch
The Square, Tel: 400
Apr–Sep. C: Masonic Building
Dounreay
Tel: Reay 203. Jun–Sep
C: Wick
Dunbeath
Laidhay Croft Folk Museum,
Tel: 275. June–Sep. C: Wick
Dunoon
Pier Esplanade, Tel: 3785
Durness
Tel: 259. Mid May–Sep
C: Dornoch
Evanton
Tel: 228. Mid Jun–mid Sep
C: Muir of Ord
Fort Augustus
Car Park, Tel: 367. May–Sep
C: Inverness
Fort William
Tel: 2232
Gairloch
Achtercairn, Tel: 2130
Glencoe
Claymore Filling Station,
Tel: Ballachulish 296
May–Sep
C: Fort William
Glenfinnan Monument (NTS)
Glenfinnan, Tel: Kinlocheil
250. Mid Apr–mid Oct
Glenshiel
Tel: 266. Jun–Sep
C: Gairloch
Golspie
Tel: 417. Mid May–mid Sep
Grantown-on-Spey
The Square, Tel: 2773
May–Sep
Helmsdale
Dunrobin Street, Tel: 640
Mid May–Sep. C: Dornoch
Inveraray
Tel: 2663. Apr–Sep
C: Campbeltown
Inverewe Gardens (NTS)

Poolewe, Tel: 229
Apr–mid Oct
Inverness
23 Church Street, Tel: 34353
Kingussie
26 High Street, Tel: 297
May–Sep
Kinlochewe
Tel: 238. Jun–Sep
C: Gairloch
Kirkwall, Orkney Is.
Mounthoolie Lane, Tel: 2856
Kyle of Lochalsh
Tel: Kyle 4276. May–Oct.
C: Gairloch
Lairg
Lairg Library, Tel: 2160
Mid May–Sep. C: Dornoch
Lerwick, Shetland Is.
Alexandra Wharf, Tel: 3434
**Lochboisdale, Isle of
South Uist,** Tel: 288. May–Sep.
C: Stornoway
Lochcarron
Tel: 317. Jun–Sep. C: Gairloch
Lochgilphead,
Tel: 2344. Apr–Sep.
C: Campbeltown County
Offices, Tel: 2177
Lochinver
Tel: 330. Mid May–Sep
C: Dornoch
**Lochmaddy,
Isle of North Uist,** Tel: 321
May–Sep. C: Stornoway
Mallaig
Tel: 2170. May–Sep
C: Fort William
Melvich
Tel: 255. Mid May–Sep
C: Dornoch
Muir or Ord
Tel: 433
Nairn
Bus Station, King Street,

Tel: 2753. Jun–Sep
Newtonmore
Main Street, Tel: 253
May–Sep. C: Aviemore
North Kessock
Car Park, Tel: Kessock 373
Mid Jun–mid Sep. C: Muir of Ord
Oban
Albany Street, Tel: 3122/2466
Portree, Isle of Skye
Meall House, Tel: 137
Stornoway, Isle of Lewis
South Beach Quay, Tel: 3088
Strathpeffer
The Square, Jun–Sep. C: Muir
of Ord
Stromness, Orkney Islands
The Pier, Tel: 491. Jun–Sep
C: Kirkwall
Tarbert (Argyll)
Tel: 429. Apr–Sep
C: Campbeltown
Tarbert, Isle of Harris
Tel: Harris 2011. May–Sep
C: Stornoway
Tarvie
Tel: Strathpeffer 575. Jun–Sep
C: Muir of Ord
Thurso
Car Park, Riverside, Tel: 2371
May–Oct. C: Wick
Tighnabruaich
Tel: 393. Apr–Sep. C: Dunoon
Tobermory, Isle of Mull
48 Main Street, Tel: 2182
Apr–Sep. C: Oct–Mar
Torridon (NTS)
Tel: 221. May–Sep
Ullapool
Tel: 2135. May–Oct
C: Gairloch
Wick
Whitechapel Road, Tel: 2596
Jun–Sep

RESORTS, ISLANDS AND PLACES OF INTEREST

In 1975, mainly for administrative purposes, Scotland was divided into new regions under the Local Government (Scotland) Act of 1973. These new regions are: Highland, Grampian, Tayside, Fife, Lothian, Central, Borders, Strathclyde, Dumfries and Galloway, Orkney, Shetland, Western Isles. In the gazetteer section which follows, at the head of main entries, you will see in italics the name of the relevant region.

Gruinard Bay (left)   *Ben Loyal, Sutherland (below)*

ABERDEEN (pop. 212,000)
Grampian the granite city, is the third largest city of Scotland and its biggest tourist resort. It is also the centre for the development of Scotland's North Sea oil industry. It lies on the rivers Dee and Don, and between them are 3 km (2 ml) of sand which account for its popularity as a family vacation centre. Children are especially well catered for at the beach which offers all the traditional pleasures, and the city also has five golf courses and is an excellent touring centre, particularly for the Braemar area. Fast train services connect it with Edinburgh and Glasgow to the south and Inverness to the north.

If you think of Aberdeen as being merely a large city with a beach, you do it a great injustice. If you keep to Union Street, the long shopping centre which bisects the city, you will miss 90 per cent of the city's charm. The shops certainly are excellent, and many visitors retain a lasting impression of the carillon of 48 bells which ring out psalms most beautifully from the belfry of the **Parish Church of St Nicholas** in Union Street. But leave this busy street by descending Back Wynd steps, past the railway station and bus station, after a short distance turn left, and you are at Trinity Quay where big ships are tied up at the streetside. The gulls wheeling and screaming over the city remind you that this city of contrasts—historic, gracious, cultured, a tourist resort and a shopping centre—is also a city of the sea. Its biggest attraction—some time around 7 in the morning!—is the **Fish Market** which is well worth the early rise. Large catches of every kind of fish are landed early in the day and auctioned to buyers—a most fascinating sight. The auctioneer's words at machine gun speed and the buyers' barely perceptible bids make a normal auction seem like something in slow motion. Guided tours can be arranged at the kiosk in the market.

To take in a good many of the sights in one day, start at the east end of Union Street and make for the mecca of all American tourists, **St Andrew's Episcopal Cathedral** in King Street. Do not look for a vast imposing building; St Andrew's stands level with the shops and is fairly unattractive from the outside. Being an Episcopal cathedral it is open on weekdays, and its attraction for Americans is that it was at the Cathedral of St Andrew's that Bishop Seabury was consecrated by the Scottish Episcopal Bishops in 1784. He then returned to America and introduced to the American Church a liturgy founded on the same model as the Scottish (based on the Greek Liturgy of St Chrysostom). Americans will therefore find the service here more familiar than will English visitors.

The interior is extremely beautiful. Americans have contributed much to its upkeep, and the Stars and Stripes is prominent. The white interior of the Cathedral is decorated in vivid blue and gold, and a great gold pillared canopy stands over the altar. The effect is one of great light and tranquillity. If you are in Aberdeen at a weekend, try to attend the Sunday evening service when the choir is at its best.

Continue from St Andrew's to nearby **Marischal College,** just a few minutes' walk away in Broad Street. This 19th-century building is an outstanding example of granite used at its finest. Marischal was founded in 1593, and is one of the two colleges of Aberdeen University. Although one of the largest granite buildings in the world, the pale grey of the stone saves this elaborate Gothic pinnacled frontage from being overwhelming. The museum part is open to the public.

Opposite Marischal is **Provost Skene's House,** a 16th-century mansion which once belonged to a wealthy merchant and provost of the city. The house and garden are open. The 17th-century tempera paintings on the timber vaults of the long gallery lay hidden behind plasterwork for 300 years until they were discovered when the house was being restored by the town council in 1951.

From Broad Street, take a bus the short distance to Old Aberdeen, getting off at **King's College,** the other of the two university colleges, and possibly the more beautiful. The college is unmistakable, for it is a gracious creeper-clad building surmounted by a 17th-century crown tower (only this tower and the chapel remain of the original building). It is fronted by a lawn with trees, and the atmosphere is tranquil and learned.

From here it is best to wander at will, for Old Aberdeen has some of the finest old Scottish houses in the country. One must be grateful to Aberdeen University for having taken over the entire area of Old Aberdeen and maintaining so many lovely buildings. The new buildings —faculty buildings and students' halls of residence—form an interesting contrast. Continue past King's College to the High Street, and squarely in your path stands the 18th-century **Old Town House,** now a branch of Aberdeen Public

Libraries. Its clean straight lines have much dignity, and it preserves an air of community in the area. Down the street called Chanonry you will pass such jewels as **Mitchell's Hospital**—a tiny courtyard with low buildings of great charm and dignity on three sides, originally built for the widows and families of the trade burgesses of Old Aberdeen.

A little further brings you to **St Machar's Cathedral,** the original church here having been founded, it is said, by St Machar on instructions from St Columba who told him to build a church when he came to a place where the river bent in the form of a shepherd's crook. Note heraldic ceiling of painted oak and the attractive modern stained glass windows.

Bordering St Machar's is **Seaton Park,** a pleasant place to rest, as are all the parks. Aberdeen is well endowed in this respect and can be justly proud of the glorious displays of flowers in all of them. The bus from Old Town House will take you back to the centre of the city.

This tour still leaves many sights unseen. There is the **Art Gallery** on Schoolhill, just behind Union Street. There the Jacob Epstein heads in the sculpture hall are worth a visit, as are the Dégas dancers and a Henry Moore. Amongst the pictures there are a Monet, a couple of Sisleys and an Augustus John, but the gallery is strongest in its display of modern Scottish painters. This is an extremely well chosen little collection. Especially endearing is one of the late Joan Eardley's street urchin pictures. Another old mansion (1594) worth seeing is **Provost Ross's House** in Shiprow. While in the area there are several whisky distilleries that can be visited—referred to locally as going on 'the whisky trail'. The local tourist office will give you details. For the antiques enthusiast, apart from browsing around the city's antique shops, there is always the possibility of a find amid the junk of the Friday second-hand market in Justice Street.

Children in particular will be fascinated by **Rubislaw Quarry** to the west of the city on the A944. At 130 m (425 ft) it is the deepest in Britain, and has supplied much of the granite for Aberdeen's buildings. **Haddo House,** north of the city just beyond Ellon, the Georgian home of the Earls of Aberdeen, has a theatre where concerts and operas are regularly performed. *Braemar 93 km/58 ml; Carlisle 338/210; Edinburgh 188/117; Glasgow 229/142; Perth 130/81; Stirling 185/115.*

ABERFELDY (pop. 1500), *Perthshire/Tayside* is a small Highland town on the River Tay offering a 9-hole golf course and grand fishing. The attractive bridge across the river was built in 1733 by General Wade in the course of his road building activities throughout Scotland (he was directly responsible for at least 378 km/235 ml) while pacifying the Highlands after the rising of 1715, and the bridge is one of his finest. That famous Scottish regiment, the Black Watch (so-called because it was charged to 'watch upon the braes' and wore a dark tartan), was mustered here, and a monument on Wade's bridge commemorates this. Aberfeldy is principally a

touring centre for the lovely Loch Tay area.

It is a short run by car or bus to the model village of **Kenmore** (10 km/6 ml) on the eastern end of Loch Tay, with its attractive white cottages lined up at the gates of Taymouth Castle. *Callander 69 km/43 ml; Perth 50/31; Pitlochry 23/14.*

ABERFOYLE (pop. 1200), *Perthshire/Tayside* Those who have read Sir Walter Scott's *Rob Roy* may wish to stop awhile at the Bailie Nicol Jarvie Hotel at Aberfoyle, nowadays a crowded tourist centre for the Trossachs. The town today offers pony trekking, golf, fishing and fine walking. The Duke's Road (built by a Duke of Montrose), leads over the Trossachs to Loch Achray and to Loch Katrine, then to Loch Vennacher, settings for Scott's *Lady of the Lake,* to Callander. Another road leads up past Lochs Ard and Chon to **Stronachlachar** on Loch Katrine whence a path leads to Glen Gyle and the house where Rob Roy was born in 1671. *Edinburgh 90 km/56 ml; Glasgow 48/30; Stirling 32/20.*

ABOYNE (pop. 2269), *Aberdeenshire/Grampian* **Ballater** and **Aboyne** are both holiday resorts with golf courses, and excellent walking country. Both hold annual games, Ballater in August and Aboyne in September. You are not far away here from a very lovely castle that is worth seeing. **Craigievar** dates from 1626 and stands off the A980 between Aboyne and Alford, and is worth

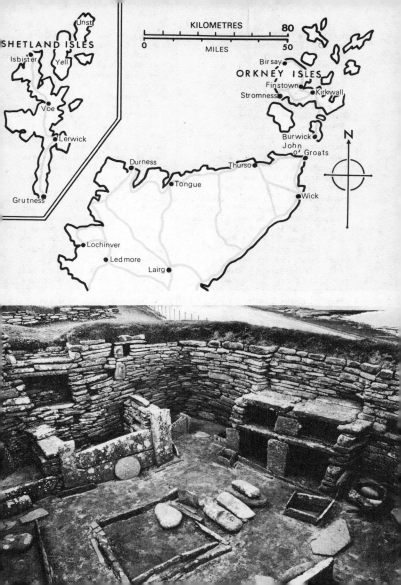

the visit for the beautifully decorated plaster ceilings alone. *Braemar to Ballater 26 km/16 ml; to Aboyne 43/27.*

ANSTRUTHER See EAST NEUK

ARBROATH (pop. 23,000), *Angus/ Tayside* Formerly known as *Aberbrothock* or 'The Mouth of the Brothock', this is a busy little town popular with family holidaymakers. There is a small harbour, golf course and open air swimming pool, and one can take boat trips up the coast. What remains of the 13th-century **Abbey**, where the Declaration of Scottish Independence was signed by Robert Bruce in 1320, is impressive. In 1950, the Stone of Scone was symbolically concealed here for a brief period. The circular window in the south transept is known as the 'O of Arbroath', and used to be lit up at night as a mark for ships. At **Kellie Castle,** 4 km (2½ ml) west of Arbroath, the old library has been converted to a gallery of contemporary Scottish art.

There is a sandy beach to the south, and to the north is some fine red cliff scenery. 'Arbroath Smokies', a form of smoked fish, are celebrated. *Aberdeen 80 km/50 ml; Dundee 26/16; Edinburgh 111/ 69; Glasgow 148/92.*

ARDRISHAIG (pop. 1000), *Argyll/ Strathclyde* Ardrishaig and its neighbour, **Lochgilphead** (3 km/2 ml), were once centres of the herring fishing industry. They now rely on tourism. Ardrishaig lies at the Loch Fyne end of the Crinan Canal which connects with the Sound of Jura and the Atlantic, and is much visited for its beauty. Those with a keen sense of history

may like to visit **Dunadd Fort** (W of A816, 6 km/4 ml NNW of Lochgilphead) for there on a hillock was once the capital of our ancient land. Kings were said to be made at the carved figure of a boar on the highest rock.

Both resorts offer fishing, boating and bathing; regular steamer services connect with the Clyde and Campbeltown. On the east shore of Loch Sween look out for **Castle Sween** which dates from the 12th century. *Glasgow 135 km/ 84 ml; Inveraray 39/24; Oban 60/37.*

ARDROSSAN (pop. 10,867), *Ayrshire/Strathclyde* Clyde coast resort, adjoining **Saltcoats.** There is a small ruined castle above the town, but most of the interest lies in the harbour from which boats leave for Arran. There is a bird sanctuary nearby at Horse Island. At Saltcoats there is a Maritime Museum by the harbour, and also the North Ayrshire Museum which shows industrial development of the area. *Irvine 10 km/6 ml; Glasgow 51/32.*

ARRAN, Isle of, *Bute/Strathclyde* It would be a pity not to see some of Scotland's wealth of islands, but if only two had to be selected I would suggest Iona as a representative of the Hebrides and Arran as a lowland island.

Arran is a large island (some 518 sq km/200 sq ml) lying in the Firth of Clyde 23 km (14 ml) from the mainland, and is reached by steamer from Ardrossan (connected by rail to Glasgow) to Brodick. A car ferry also operates between Ardrossan and Brodick. A good local bus service enables the visitor to travel around the island easily, and there are bus touring facilities in operation. The scenery is spectacular. A road circles the island, and another one crosses it from east to west, from Brodick to Blackwaterfoot.

Main towns are **Brodick** (pop. 500)—from where one can climb Goatfell (875 m/2866 ft) with a magnificent view of Scotland, England and Ireland, or enjoy golf, tennis, bowling and fine sands—**Lochranza, Lamlash** and **Whiting Bay,** all with similar amenities. **Brodick Castle** and gardens are open to the public. There are in fact two gardens, one formal which dates from 1710, and the other, said to be one of the finest rhododendron gardens in the country. Pleasure cruisers are based on Brodick.

ARROCHAR (pop. 700), *Dunbarton./ Strathclyde* Arrochar occupies a very sheltered site at the head of Loch Long on the road over the 'Rest and Be Thankful' to Inveraray. It is a surprisingly untidy village in a beautiful setting, much given to 'tartanalia' and tea rooms. The former is unfortunate, the latter no doubt necessary to cope with the weekend influx of motorists. This is not a place to get away from tourists and their litter. A 3 km (2 ml) walk or bus ride takes one over to **Tarbet** on Loch Lomond along roughly the same route that must have been followed, in 1263, by some of King Haakon's men who dragged their ships across to Loch Lomond and launched them there—a magnificent if futile feat.

Arrochar is a climbers' centre, and mountaineers can tackle Ben Arthur (880 m/2891 ft), better known as 'The Cobbler', which rises above the village looking as though some giant had nibbled around its craggy peak. *Glasgow 60 km/38 ml; Inveraray 35/22.*

AVIEMORE (pop. 1200), *Inverness./ Highland* Long a well-known centre for the attractive South Spey area, the skiing boom has now transformed Aviemore into a continental-type sports village. It has new hotels and shops, and is the centre of major tourist development. You can canoe, sail, climb, hill walk, ski (there is an artificial slope for novices), skate, fish, go-kart, glide, or play curling, depending on the season. Don't fail to visit the visually exciting, historically accurate Landmark Centre at **Carrbridge,** with its restaurant, nature trail, and (in summer) evening film programmes. At Loch Garten Nature Reserve you can watch ospreys from the Observation Post 13 km (8 ml) NE of Aviemore.

Within reach is Glenmore National Forest Park which is a wonderful area in which to let children come to grips with nature. A chair lift ascends almost to the top of the Cairngorm 1255 m (4084 ft). Ask locally about the Strathspey railway. This is being renovated by enthusiasts of steam railways and it runs from Boat of Garten to Aviemore. Off an unclassified road from B970, 19 km (12 ml) SSW of Aviemore is the 3-km (2-ml) circular Achlean Nature Trail with observation tower. *Inverness 50 km/31 ml; Perth 138/86.*

AYR (pop. 48,000), *Ayrshire/ Strathclyde* Ayr is something of an all-round town. For children its special attractions are 3 km (2 ml) of safe, sandy beach, an ice rink, a boating pond, a large indoor swimming pool, and an amusement park at Foreshore. For sports 51

Glamis Castle (above)   *Charlotte Square, Edinburgh (below)*

enthusiasts it offers a famous race course, three golf courses, tennis, bowling and boating on the River Ayr. There is no lack of summer entertainment and, for the Burns enthusiast it is the centre of the poet's country. The Tam o' Shanter Inn in the High Street is now a Burns Museum and he was baptized in the Auld Kirk (1655) in 1759. Three km (2 ml) away at **Alloway** is the cottage where he was born, with manuscripts and the family Bible on view. Almost 1 km ($\frac{1}{2}$ ml) on is the Brig o' Doon which saved Tam o' Shanter in his flight from the witches, as they were unable to cross running water. Those on a Burns pilgrimage may want to take in **Tarbolton,** 12 km (7$\frac{1}{2}$ ml) NE of Ayr (B744) where the Bachelors' Club, founded by Burns and his friends as a literary and debating society, housed in a 17th-century house, is open to the public on request.

But this is only one side of Ayr. There is the late medieval **Auld Brig** which offers delightful passage across the river, and the 16th-century **Loudon Hall,** formerly the residence of the Sheriffs of Ayrshire, has been beautifully restored. Ayr is also an industrial town, an agricultural centre and a fishing port, all of which ensure that it retains its bustling, prosperous atmosphere even after the summer visitors have gone. Robert Adam's splendid **Culzean Castle** lies 19 km (12 ml) SSW of Ayr and should not be missed. In 1946 the top flat was given to the late General Eisenhower as a Scottish residence in a token of appreciation. The grounds of the Castle are now a Country Park and include a walled garden established in 1783, an aviary, swan pond and camellia house. *Dumfries 98 km/61 ml; Glasgow 53/33; Carlisle 148/92.*

BALLACHULISH (pop. 1254), *Argyll./Highland* Not a pretty village, having once been a centre of the slate industry, but the surrounding scenery is magnificent. There is a bridge (built in 1975), cross it and from there continue the drive south through the beautiful scenery of Appin to Oban, or else branch east and take the famous route through Glencoe. It was at Appin that the murder of Colin Campbell of Glenure took place, and this event formed the basis of Robert Louis Stevenson's book *Kidnapped. Fort William 26 km/16$\frac{1}{2}$ ml.*

BALLATER See ABOYNE

BANFF (pop. 4000), *Banff./Grampian* A beautiful and historic little town with **Macduff** its sister town and important herring fishing centre, on the opposite bank of the River Deveron. It has some interesting old houses and buildings, particularly from the 17th and 18th centuries (**The Town House** and **St Mary's Church**), good bus services and sporting facilities. Close by the Town House is the **Biggar Fountain** where an outlaw, James Macpherson, played his fiddle to the crowd before his execution in 1701. By Carmelite Street—a reminder that there was a monastery here as early as the 12th century—stands a fine **Mercat** (Market) **Cross.**

Duff House, formerly owned by the Duke of Fife and presented to the two towns in 1906, has extensive grounds which offer tennis and golf. It is generally held to be William Adam's masterpiece (brother of the more celebrated Robert), and is modelled on the Villa Borghese in

Rome. From the grounds a path runs by the side of the river to the picturesque gorge at **Bridge of Alvah.** All along this coast is an area of cliff and sand, and one is always aware of the sea. *Aberdeen 96 km/60 ml; Inverness 119/74.*

BARRA, Isle of, *Inverness./ Western Isles* The islands of Barra and Eriskay form the most southerly section of the Outer Hebrides. (Nearby **Eriskay** is known by a beautiful song *The Eriskay Love Lilt,* and this tiny island of fisherfolk can be reached by small boat from Lochboisdale in South Uist.)

Barra is the happy island of the Hebrides. It is a Catholic island, quite different in temperament and scenery from the nothern islands of the Outer Hebrides. It is reached by regular boat service from Mallaig and Oban to Castlebay, the 'township' of the island—a scattered village with a splendid new hotel opened in 1974, and some guesthouse accommodation. It is a lovely spot to sail into because Kisimul Castle, a small romantic looking castle, perches on a tiny islet right in the middle of the bay. It is a gift for photographers. Parts of the castle date from the 11th century, and it was the seat of the MacNeils of Barra. It fell into near ruin, but was restored in recent years by the then chief of the MacNeils, an American; it can be visited on Saturdays.

The most delightful thing about Barra is the feeling of happiness generated by the islanders. (This is the island on which the film *Whisky Galore* was made.) They will tell you a tall story in their delightful lilting voices or invite you to a local dance. It doesn't matter if you are a stranger, the Barra folk are naturally friendly and great conversationalists. You won't be there more than a day before half the island knows all about you.

If you enjoy walking, there is a road right round the island—22 km (14 ml). You will pass rocky scenery on the eastern side and surely Britain's most beautiful beaches on the west. In the middle of the island is Ben Heaval, over 366 m (1200 ft).

The planes come in at North Bay, not on a normal airstrip but upon a cocklestrand on the beach. It is quite exciting to witness this, and perfectly safe for those planning to fly to Barra, for the beach is hard packed and finely ground shell, a natural phenomenon.

BRAEMAR (pop. 500), *Aberdeen./ Grampian* Quite definitely on the tourist beat, Braemar is the most westerly of a string of villages along the banks of the Dee which earn a livelihood from tourism, engendered by the scenic attractions of the area and their proximity to Balmoral Castle, summer home of the Royal Family.

Braemar's dilemma is that it has to please every kind of tourist, and thus it is an unhappy mixture of shops selling cheap souvenirs, good craftwork and excellent antiques. Nonetheless, it is a pretty little village standing 335 m (1100 ft) above sea level, surrounded by wooded hills, and has dry, bracing air. Robert Louis Stevenson spent many months here while writing *Treasure Island,* and his cottage is marked with a plaque.

The big annual social event is the Royal Braemar Gathering held in September, which the Queen and Royal Family always attend. It has been a royal occasion since 1848. Here you will see traditional games with plenty of piping and the tossing of the caber, all in beautiful surroundings and with the added excitement of its being a royal event.

Within walking distance of the village (3 km/1½ ml) is **Braemar Castle,** open to the public, which was one of the garrisons used to keep the Highlanders in check after the rising of 1715. The *Invercauld Arms Hotel* now stands on the spot where the Earl of Mar raised the standard in 1715.

This area is one which should be seen in autumn when the colours are magnificent. No wonder Queen Victoria loved it! **Balmoral Castle** was built by her consort, Prince Albert. It is of white granite in the 'Scottish Baronial' style, and is often described nowadays as a 'great Victorian pile', but it has its attractions. There are many smaller imitations of the style scattered all over Deeside. When the Queen is not in residence, some of the grounds of Balmoral are open to the public.

The most beautiful part of the road is from Braemar to Balmoral, passing the little church of **Crathie** (attended by the Royal Family when in residence at Balmoral). In September when the bracken is turning to yellow and gold, the roadside vibrates with colour, for the green of the grass mixes with the purple of the heather and the golden bracken. In winter this is skiing country. There is a chairlift at Glenshee (16 km/10 ml S of Braemar) up Cairnwell mountain. *Aberdeen 93 km/58 ml; Edinburgh 188/117; Glasgow 229/142; Inverness 129/80.*

CALLANDER (pop. 2000), *Perthshire/Central* A good touring centre for the Trossachs, one of the most popular areas in Scotland, Callander has a wide variety of accommodation as well as facilities for golf, tennis, bowls, climbing (Ben Ledi, 875 m/2875 ft, but not a difficult climb) and fishing. Nearby are the **Bracklinn Falls** on the River Keltie, and the **Falls of Leny** where a large volume of water is forced through a narrow cutting in the rock and the River Leny turns into a boiling cauldron. Callander itself stands on the Teith just below its junction with the Leny.

A footpath from the main street of Callander leads to the remains of a Roman Camp.

Sir Walter Scott's poem *The Lady of the Lake* first made the **Trossachs** famous, and indeed the whole of this area is associated with his novels. Basically, the Trossachs is the area around the pass between Loch Achray and Loch Katrine. To the north rises Ben A'an, and Ben Venue (730 m/2393 ft) lies to the south. The whole area is richly wooded and very picturesque. A steamer sails daily up Loch Katrine to Stronachlachar past Ellen's Island, where the marauding Macgregors used to keep their stolen cattle, and to Ben Venue. Rob Roy, the most infamous of the Macgregors, is buried at Balquhidder churchyard (22 km/14 ml from Callander). *Edinburgh 82 km/51 ml; Glasgow 58/36; Stirling 43/27.*

CAMPBELTOWN (pop. 6500), *Argyll./Strathclyde* Campbeltown is the only town on that long arm of land called Kintyre which, were it not for the isthmus of Tarbert, would be an island and part of the Hebrides. In the 17th century the town was granted to the Campbells of Argyll, and took its name from

them. Once it was a centre of the
herring fishing industry, but when
the herring shoals mysteriously
left our coasts, Campbeltown
turned to other industries.
Tourism was one of them, and there
is a rocky beach and good sea
angling, as well as a small·harbour
from which Flora MacDonald,
sailed to Carolina in 1774.

The golf course of **Machrihanish**
is nearby, and there is also an
airport there with services to
Glasgow and Islay. There is much
evidence of early settlement on
Kintyre. In Campbeltown itself a
15th-century Celtic cross, richly
carved, stands at Old Quay Head,
and at **Achinoan Head** (5 km/3 ml)
is St Kieran's Cave which may be
the earliest Christian chapel in
Scotland. At the village of
Southend on the tip of Kintyre,
St Columba is reputed to have
landed for the first time in
Scotland, and a local legend has
it that his footprints may be seen
near Dunaverty Castle.

Regular steamer services connect
Campbeltown with the island of
Arran and the Clyde.

The village of **Carradale** (21 km/
13 ml) NNE of Campbeltown) is the
start of several forestry walks, and
there also are the gardens of
Carradale House (home of writer
Naomi Mitchison) which are open
to the public. *Glasgow 214 km/134
ml; Lochgilphead 82/51; Oban
142/88.*

CRAIL See EAST NEUK

CRIEFF (pop. 5500), *Perth./Tayside*
Set against a backdrop of hills,
Crieff is a sheltered touring centre
in the traditional style, with fishing
and golfing facilities. The Knock
(278 m/911 ft), a wooded hill, sits
above the town with the Hydro

Hotel before it, seeming to preside
over the steep streets of Crieff.

In front of the Town Hall note
the very old weather-worn cross
and the iron stocks which were in
use until 1816. Walk a little further
up the main street and on the
opposite side, behind railings, you
will see the ancient Burgh Cross,
a Celtic cross of about the 10th
century. **Macrosty Park** is well
laid out, but the town is well
placed for longer walks.

On Wednesdays, from April to
September, **Abercairny gardens**
are open to the public (off A85,
7 km/4½ ml ENE of Crieff) and
they are specially noted for fine
azaleas and rhododendron. Another
notable garden open to the public
is that of **Drummond Castle** (on
Wednesdays and Saturdays, April
to mid-August). It stands off the
A8022 about 4 km (2½ ml) south
of Crieff.

This is a good touring centre,
for from here on the scenery gets
better all the time. The colouring
in autumn of the Sma' Glen is
exceptional, and there are Roman
remains to be seen. **Gleneagles** is
only 14 km (9 ml) away. The
scenery around Gleneagles is not
particularly attractive but that is
of little importance because
enthusiasts come here primarily to
golf. *Gleneagles Hotel* provides well
for its international clientele and
the courses (King's and Queen's)
are excellent. Make sure your
wallet is well filled before entering
this hotel—it is very expensive.

Ochtertyre Theatre in the
home of Sir William Murray, the
18th-century Ochtertyre House,
just outside Crieff, presents elegant
and intimate theatre, and is a
welcome addition to the cultural
life of the area.

Another pleasant tour from

Crieff can be made to the village of **Comrie** 8 km (5 ml) which in the past has been subject to earthquakes—none of them serious—because it lies directly on the 'Highland fault'. It is a straggling, pretty village and there is good walking in the district. *Edinburgh 106 km/66 ml; Perth 27/17; Stirling 48/30.*

DINGWALL (pop. 4000), *Ross and Cromarty/Highland* Said to have been created a Royal Burgh in 1226, the town has an important mart, or market, one of the largest schools in the north, Dingwall Academy, and is important to the tourist primarily as the starting point of the routes to the north. With ample accommodation, it is a good touring centre, and in the High Street there are the remains of an old Mercat Cross and an iron yett or gate from the old town prison.

At **Cromarty** (26 km/16 ml NE of Dingwall) can be seen the birthplace of Hugh Miller, the eminent geologist of the 19th century. *Inverness 39 km/24 ml; Lochinver 135/84; Thurso 217/135; Ullapool 74/46.*

DORNOCH (pop. 1000), *Sutherland/ Highland* The combination of this little Royal Burgh of extensive golf links and great stretches of sandy beach makes it an ideal family vacation spot. This combination continues north encompassing **Golspie** (16 km/10 ml) and **Brora** (27 km/17 ml)—a healthy, invigorating area for children and parents alike. There are two golf courses at Dornoch, one, The Royal Dornoch, is very famous.

Dornoch itself is an attractive little town. There is a 13th-century Cathedral (now the Parish Church),

and the remains of Dornoch Castle (once the bishop's palace, for Dornoch was the seat of the Bishops of Caithness) have been turned into a hotel. It is in good walking country and makes an excellent motoring centre. **Skibo Castle** (about 6 km/4 ml west) once belonged to Andrew Carnegie, and parts of **Dunrobin Castle** (near Golspie), date back to 1275 or so. This is impressive looking even from the roadway (A9), and the castle gardens are open in summer. *Aberdeen 254 km/158 ml; Glasgow 349/217; Inverness 87/54; Nairn 113/70; Ullapool 100/62.*

DOUNE (pop. 762), *Perthshire/ Central* 5 km (3 ml) west of Dunblane, formerly famous for the pistols manufactured there. Visit **Doune Castle,** where out of season I was given a large key and a lamp, both necessary to get you into and up the winding stairways of this very well preserved 14th-century castle. There is a keeper on duty during the summer. In the centre of the castle is a fine medieval courtyard. Just outside the village is a Motor Museum, and at nearby **Blair Drummond** an African Safari Park where lions, giraffes, zebras and other animals can be seen in 'natural' surroundings. Doune lies on the road to Callander and the beautiful hills of the Trossachs. *Stirling 14 km/9 ml.*

DUMFRIES (pop. 29,000), *Dumfries./Dumfries and Galloway* Largest and most important town in the south of Scotland, Dumfries is the main industrial and educational centre of the area. Sir J. M. Barrie, creator of *Peter Pan,* went to school at Dumfries Academy.

In Burns Street can be seen the

house where Robert Burns lived after he had unsuccessfully farmed for three years at **Ellisland** (10 km/6 ml north). The house contains relics and manuscripts and is open to the public. Robert Burns, his wife Jean Armour, and their sons are buried in St Michael's churchyard nearby. Across the River Nith at **Maxwelltown** is an 18th-century windmill, now a regional museum housing Roman and early Christian relics and a collection of local costumes.

Dumfries offers golfing on two courses, boating and fishing and from Ae Forest Office (W from A701, 16 km/10 ml N of Dumfries) walks can be taken through the forest. There is a small forest museum and picnic site there. At **Caerlaverock** (14 km/9 ml S of Dumfries) there is a fine castle to be seen, and wildfowl on the nature reserve there. *Carlisle 51 km/32 ml; Edinburgh 117/73; Glasgow 119/74.*

DUNBAR (pop. 4553), *East Lothian/Lothian* From the main road this seems like any other east coast town but you must go into the town and drop down to the harbour to see the most attractive part. The remains of its ancient castle almost enclose the harbour in a most picturesque way. The harbour area itself is a jumble of old buildings crying out for sensitive redevelopment. The **Town House** in the main street dates from 1620 but otherwise there is little of architectural interest in the shopping part of the town, though part of the Myreton Motor Museum is at **Castle Park** at the end of the High Street (the other part is near **Aberlady**, off the A198).

There is a much painted and photographed old watermill in the area—**Preston Mill**—said to be the only one still in working order. It lies about 10 km (6 ml) west of Dunbar, near East Linton, and there is a good example, also nearby, in Phantassie Doocot of an old Scottish dovecot (the birds were kept as a winter supply of food). *Edinburgh 46 km/29 ml.*

DUNBLANE (pop. 4921), *Perthshire/Central* A cathedral town with a 16th-century bridge spanning the Allan Water, it lies 8 km (5 ml) north on the Perth road from Stirling. The 12th-century **Cathedral** has been restored, and there is a delightful little chapel at the west end. *Stirling 8 km/5 ml.*

DUNDEE (pop. 184,000), *Angus/Tayside* Dundee is primarily an industrial and commercial city, famous for generations as the city of 'jute, jam and journalism'. Now when the basic industries of Scotland are undergoing drastic changes—this trio still remains true to Dundee with the addition of several new light industries.

The road bridge will interest those with an engineering bent. Not as impressive as the Forth Road Bridge, it is just as effective, for it is now possible to travel in a straight line from Edinburgh to Dundee instead of taking the old car ferry across the Firth of Tay or making a detour, as one formerly had to, via Perth.

The **Howff** is notable, a quaint burying ground gifted to the town by Mary, Queen of Scots, and the **Old Steeple** (48 m/156 ft) should be seen. It dates from the 14th century and crowns the city churches, three churches under one roof. **Caird Park** has two golf courses (one 18-hole), tennis courts and bowling greens, and the remains of Claverhouse Castle.

Queen's College, for long part of the University of St Andrews, became a university in its own right in 1967. The art gallery in Albert Square has some good Scottish pictures.

Nearby (6 km/4 ml east) is **Broughty Ferry,** a popular little seaside resort, with its restored Broughty Castle (early 16th-century) which has a museum of whaling. At Beach Crescent, the Orchard Gallery has a good collection of Scottish pictures.

At **Camperdown,** see the Spalding Golf Museum; at **Claypotts Castle** is one of the most complete of the old turreted tower houses; and try not to miss the *Unicorn* in Victoria Dock, the oldest British-built ship afloat. It is a 46-gun wooden frigate of 1824 and is open to view. *Aberdeen 105 km/65 ml; Braemar 87/54; Edinburgh 85/53; Perth 35/22.*

DUNFERMLINE (pop. 50,000), *Fife* This ancient Royal Burgh is not in itself the most beautiful of towns. It is extremely hilly and many of the main streets are too narrow to be able to cope efficiently with present day traffic. It has two big attractions, **Dunfermline Abbey** and **Pittencrieff Glen.** The latter was gifted to the town by Andrew Carnegie, the Scottish-American philanthropist, who was born in a small house there (open to the public) in 1835. He was especially generous to his own town and left money for the development and upkeep of the glen which has wooded walks, flower gardens and a museum. The first of his 2,500 libraries is in Appin Crescent. Built in 1881, it contains many treasures.

The Abbey can be seen from a distance rather in the manner of

Durham Cathedral, and is a handsome structure. It was founded in the 11th century by King Malcolm and Queen Margaret. Seven Scottish kings are buried there—the last was King Robert I (Robert Bruce) who was buried in the choir, and over this part rises a great square tower. Around the top of the tower in large stone letters is his name 'King Robert the Bruce', forming a kind of balustrade.

Since the building of the Forth Road Bridge this ancient linen producing town is busier than ever. Excellent bus services radiate from the sizeable bus station. *Edinburgh 26 km/16 ml; Glasgow 63/39; Perth 48/30.*

DUNKELD (pop. 1000), *Perthshire/ Tayside* This little town owes its charm to the restoration work done by the National Trust for Scotland. Much of the ancient **Cathedral,** built over a period spanning the 14th to the 16th centuries, still remains and indeed the choir is still used as the parish church. Around it the delightful little houses in the High Street, Cathedral Street and the Cross belong to the National Trust which has let them to local people.

If you appreciate this kind of old Scottish atmosphere, Dunkeld would make an ideal touring centre. It lies between Pitlochry and Perth in pleasant wooded, hilly country. In the grounds of **Dunkeld House** are the absorbing remains of a prehistoric fort. About 3 km (2 ml) from Dunkeld there are three Forestry Commission walks to take at **Craigvinean** with the possibility of seeing wildcat, capercailzie and badgers. *Edinburgh 87 km/54 ml; Perth 26/16; Pitlochry 18/11.*

DUNOON (pop. 10,000), *Argyll/
Strathclyde* Dunoon and Rothesay
are probably the two most popular
Clyde resorts. Although Dunoon
is on the mainland, the most
popular route there is by a steamer
from Gourock (reached by train
from Glasgow), and therefore one
has all the atmosphere of an island
plus the amenities of a mainland
town.

Castle Hill Gardens run down
to the pier which is the centre
of interest with steamers arriving
all day long in summer. There are
two golf courses, and a few good
shops, river and loch fishing, a
bathing lido on West Bay, tennis,
bowling and boating. Dunoon is
the home of the Royal Clyde Yacht
Club and the setting for the
important Cowal Games held
annually at the end of August
(ending with the March of a
Thousand Pipers). There are
steamer connections with all the
Clyde coast towns.

The area around Dunoon is so
lovely that one must ignore the
attractions of the typical seaside
resort to see something of the area
—**Cairndow, Strachur, Otter
Ferry, Innellan.** There is a good
scenic road to **Tighnabruaich.**
Those interested in plants will
certainly want to see the Younger
Botanic Garden (on the A815, 11
km/7 ml NNW of Dunoon)—try to
make it in May or June to see the
rhododendron and azaleas. There
are plenty of cruises from Dunoon
and coach tours too if you want to
enjoy the scenery without the
worry of driving yourself. *Arrochar
64 km/40 ml; Glasgow 42/26 (ferry);
Largs 23/14 (ferry); Inveraray 63/39.*

EAST NEUK—this is a generic
name for that coast of Fife which
contains the most picturesque little

fishing ports in the country. They
run in a line—**Largo, Elie, St
Monance, Pittenweem,
Anstruther** and **Crail. St Monance**
(pop. 1400), is noted for boat
building. The harbour is a
delightful miniature and beyond
it some very attractive cottages
stand almost on the rocks. The
14th-century church, said to have
been built by David II, has been in
continuous use ever since. In the
simple interior a large model of a
ship hangs from the roof. **Largo's**
claim to fame is that it is the
birthplace of Alexander Selkirk,
the original Robinson Crusoe.
Elie is very popular as a summer
resort and has a fine golf course.
At **Anstruther,** where the shopping
street is actually on the harbour,
there is the Scottish Fisheries
Museum which aims to give some
idea of what a fisherman's life is
like. One can't help but get a sense
of the past in these villages, and
especially at **Crail.** Go up to the
castle walk for a good view back
across the old houses to the
harbour—the red pantiles, the
rugged coastline, the huge slabs
of rough-hewn stone that go to
make up the harbour, all sum up
the charm of the place. Take time
to wander around the little town
itself—the tolbooth is early 16th-
century, the church is 13th-century
and there is a delightful Mercat
Cross topped by a unicorn. There
is also a working potter in town
who welcomes visitors.

EDINBURGH (pop. 476,000),
Midlothian/Lothian Part of
Edinburgh's fame rests on its
main thoroughfare, Princes Street,
although this dates only from the
late 18th century. On one side of
the street are large shops but on
the other side, in a hollow which

used to be Nor' Loch, lie Princes Street Gardens, lovingly tended by the city gardeners, and out of this freshness there rises, sheer and rugged, the great rock on which stands **Edinburgh Castle.**

There has been a fortress of sorts on this incomparable site since Pictish times. At its highest point stands the little Norman chapel of St Margaret. South of this chapel around Palace Yard stand the Scottish National War Memorial (1927), the Old Palace (15th- and 17th-century) where the Scottish Regalia or crown jewels are displayed, Queen Mary's Apartments where James VI of Scotland was born in 1566, and the Old Parliament Hall which is now a fascinating armoury. Close by is the Halfmoon Battery from which the 1 o'clock gun is fired daily.

The road which runs from the castle esplanade, site of the Military Tattoo during the Festival, to the Queen's Scottish Palace of Holyrood House formed the nucleus of old Edinburgh. This street, popularly called the **Royal Mile** and consisting of Castle Hill, the Lawnmarket, the High Street and Canongate, was in the 17th century a dirt road flanked by tall tenements in which all the social classes lived. Just above street level were the apartments of the rich merchants and nobility, while the higher one ascended the stairs of these tall houses, the poorer became the inhabitants.

Edinburgh was a small city at that time, surrounded by protective walls. When, in the mid-18th century, a wealthy merchant decided to build a house beyond the castle moat, the townspeople regarded him as an eccentric, and it was the popular opinion that he would die of pneumonia away from

the stifling congestion of the old town. This man, however, made the first move into what became known as the New Town, a unique spread of elegant Georgian crescents, streets and squares which still survives, though the beautiful houses are now mainly used as offices. James Craig was responsible for the general layout of the New Town of which the outstanding features are possibly **Queen Street** and **Charlotte Square,** designed by Robert Adam with the imposing **St George's Church** (now the home of the nation's records). This great Scottish architect was also responsible for the old buildings of the **University** off Nicolson Street and the magnificent **Register House** at the east end of Princes Street. While in Charlotte Square don't miss the restoration of one of the finest houses (next door to the National Trust headquarters) to its Georgian state. It is one of the Trust's most imaginative projects in recent years, and dramatically conveys the graciousness of the period.

The best way to get a quick overall picture of Edinburgh is to take one of the City Transport bus tours which start from Waverley Bridge at the east end of Princes Street. They are moderately priced and a commentary is provided on all places of interest. One can thus see in comfort the main points of interest, get an idea of the geography and often a most colourful version of the history of this great city.

Edinburgh is a feast for any student of architecture, although **Princes Street** has been called an atrocity from the architectural point of view because of the amalgam of styles, classical and

bastard. When built, Princes Street had small Regency-type buildings, contrasting with the mansions of George Street and Queen Street. In the middle stands the needle-sharp monument to Sir Walter Scott. It looks like nothing so much as a 60-m (200-ft) high wedding cake, but it serves as a useful landmark for visitors who may climb the 287 steps to the top by an inside stairway. Just west of the monument, at the foot of the Mound, stand two imposing neo-classical buildings, designed by W. H. Playfair. The one bordering Princes Street is the **Royal Scottish Academy** (open daily), whose annual exhibition runs from mid-April through to autumn. In the winter months leading Scottish groups hold exhibitions there.

Many people overlook the other gallery which stands directly behind the Academy. This is the **National Gallery** (open daily, admission free), the home of Scotland's national art collection. The small but extremely well chosen collection includes famous works by the great artists of the world—Botticelli, Verrocchio, El Greco, Rembrandt, Corot, Dégas, Monet, Gauguin, Van Gogh, Picasso. The English and Scottish schools are, of course, well represented. The **Gallery of Modern Art** (open daily, admission free) is in the centre of the Botanical Gardens (buses 23, 27 from the Mound), and houses a small collection in delightful surroundings. The gallery itself is an attractive house, and around the front lawn are placed a number of sculptures, including an outstanding Henry Moore, looking strong and utterly natural in the clear northern light. There is a tea room with a few tables and chairs on the side lawn, and from

there one has one of the best views of the old city.

From Princes Street, the Mound leads into North Bank Street and up to the Royal Mile where there are many individual buildings which are worth visiting: **St Giles Church,** parts of which date from the 14th century, with its magnificent crown steeple (1495) although much of the rest of the building has been rather unfortunately restored; **John Knox's House,** timbered and gabled, and bearing the inscription over the ground floor window 'Lufe Gode abufe al and yi nyghbour as yi self'; **Huntly House Museum,** a largely reconstructed building, the original of which was 16th-century, containing relics of Burns and Scott; and **Acheson House.** This fine mansion, restored in 1937, was once the home of Sir Archibald Acheson and his wife, Dame Margaret Hamilton, whose initials are on the outside along with the Acheson crest and the date of building, 1633. Now it houses the Scottish Craft Centre, a sales outlet for the many craftsmen in remote areas of Scotland whose work is of the highest order. Acheson House gives a very good idea of the attractiveness of Scottish domestic architecture.

All over the city there are quaint corners and courtyards which make excellent subjects for the photographer, and at the foot of the Royal Mile (near Holyrood House) is a courtyard called **White Horse Close.** In the 17th century this was an inn and staging post for the Edinburgh to London coach, but it has recently been reconstructed by the town authorities, and the modern flats within the close have been rented to the public. The policy of the Edinburgh Corporation has been to reconstruct various buildings in the Royal Mile in their original style and let them, and this policy not only improves the looks and atmosphere of one of the city's most historic streets, but has also turned what had become an unsightly slum into a most attractive place to live.

The **Palace of Holyroodhouse,** together with the remains of **Holyrood Abbey,** lie at the end of the Royal Mile. Built in the 16th century, its most romantic associations are with Mary Queen of Scots, and both her apartments where Rizzio was murdered by Darnley in 1566, and Darnley's own apartments above, connected by a staircase in the wall, may be seen. The State Apartments, which are used by the present Queen, contain some beautiful tapestries and paintings, including one by Reynolds of George III and Queen Charlotte.

If you are visiting the city in a family party, there are several museums etc. which will especially interest children. The **Museum of Childhood,** almost opposite Knox's House, in the High Street, contains a large collection of toys through the ages, open Monday to Saturday and on Sundays during the Festival. The wax works are also in the High Street. The **Royal Scottish Museum,** Chambers Street, the largest science and art museum (excluding painting) in the U.K. has many working models, and is a favourite place for a wet afternoon. **Edinburgh Zoo,** situated in a very well laid out park, has a fine collection of animals and birds, the largest collection of penguins in captivity (the daily Penguins' Parade is a delight to children), and a special children's farm where the young can tend the more

domesticated animals. (Open daily.) Restaurant, cafeteria, car park. Buses westwards from Princes Street.

All children love to wait for the mechanical cuckoo to pop out when the floral clock in Princes Street Gardens strikes the quarter-hours. This is the oldest floral clock in the world, and around 24,000 dwarf plants are used. Children will also be interested in the time ball on top of the **Nelson Monument** (Calton Hill, east end of Princes Street) which drops coincidentally with the one o'clock gun.

Edinburgh's fame has, of course, been enhanced by the annual **International Festival** of Music, Drama and Art and the Film Festival. The Festival runs for three weeks from the latter part of August into early September, and every hall in the city is pressed into service, for not only does Edinburgh offer the outstanding conventional events of any such festival, but it also becomes temporarily the mecca for aspiring drama groups, choirs, artists and entertainers of every kind who form the vivacious 'Fringe'. For thousands of visitors—nearly a quarter of a million see it every year—the greatest thrill of the Festival is provided by Scottish Command's Military Tattoo, played out every evening on the floodlit esplanade with Edinburgh Castle as its backdrop. Accommodation is at a premium during the Festival, but the Edinburgh Accommodation Bureau, Market Street, will help visitors at any time of the year, and issues a free list of hotels, boarding houses etc. Booking forms can be obtained in April from the Festival Society, Market Street.

Edinburgh is surrounded by ancient little villages, now part of the city: **Cramond,** delightful, with the 16th-century **Lauriston Castle** nearby; **Duddingston,** with wildfowl on its loch; **Swanston,** with its thatched cottages beloved of Robert Louis Stevenson; and **Dean Village.** The entrance to this is only a few minutes' walk from the West End, via a lane on the city side of Dean Bridge, and once there you are removed from the flurry of the city and seem to be in a former century. The village straddles Edinburgh's river, the Water of Leith, and is a tumble of old buildings, some now being sensitively reconstructed. It is a favourite haunt of artists and photographers and of those who enjoy a quiet riverside stroll into Stockbridge (buses take you back to Princes Street in three minutes). This is the essence of Edinburgh—the old amidst the new—a city that is modern and international, yet succeeds in remaining gracious and elegant.

Edinburgh is an excellent city in which to eat out. During the Festival period, Edinburgh is bursting at her elegant seams. The wise take lunch early, before the restaurants become too crowded. Many find a favourite public house where they can have a snack and a pint of strong Scottish beer. The most popular pubs are in the centre of the city in Rose Street which runs parallel to Princes Street. Make sure you get the Scottish Tourist Board's leaflet *55 things to do in Edinburgh* so that nothing is inadvertently missed. *Aberdeen 188 km/117 ml; Berwick 92/57; Glasgow 71/44; Stirling 58/36.*

EIGG, RHUM, MUCK and **CANNA (Inner Hebrides),** *Inverness./Western Isles* These

islands can be visited as a group. Take a boat from Mallaig to **Eigg,** a long narrow strip (10 km by 6 km/ 6 ml by 4 ml) with its unmistakable *sgurr*—a high wall of cliff (393 m/1289 ft) dropping steeply at one end to the sea. There are two tiny settlements and the population (predominantly elderly) is dwindling. Do not go on chance, for there is no hotel, but a letter to the postmistress may put you in touch with someone willing to take visitors. There was only one house which did this when I stayed there and it was very comfortable. This was at **Cleadale,** very close to the singing sands of Eigg, a phenomenon known in only a few places dotted around the world. If you strike the sand sharply with the side of your hand it makes an odd singing sound.

Eigg offers perfect peace. It is an ideal place for nature lovers and ideal for children. There is one general store midway between the harbour settlement and Cleadale so that it is equally inconvenient for all. Gaelic is still spoken as well as English.

From Eigg it is possible to visit **Muck,** a tiny nearby island with a harbour at **Port Mor.** The romantic and mysterious looking island of **Rhum** is Eigg's neighbour, but it belongs to the Nature Conservancy and the public cannot land there at will. One can see all one wants, though, from the steamer—the ghastly Victorian **Kinloch Castle** (home of a past proprietor) and the wonderful mountains which are the home of red deer. But the best view of Rhum is from Eigg, framed against a blazing Hebridean sunset, when it looks too good to be true.

The contrast with **Canna** could not be greater. Tremendously fertile, this 10-km (6-ml) long

relatively flat island makes a happy impression immediately. It seems as though the entire population turns out to meet the boat. There is no hotel, but occasionally a crofter will take in visitors. There are one or two sandy bays but the coastline is mostly rocky with some caves.

ELGIN (pop. 12,300), *Moray./ Grampian* Elgin today is a bustling market town, centre of the fertile Laigh of Moray, with an attractive park (16 hectares/ 40 acres) offering the usual sporting amenities. There is a museum in the High Street, and boating on a children's pond. For those interested in architecture there are the remains of some fine buildings in the High Street and

Logan Bay, Wigtownshire

ruins of **Elgin Cathedral.** In the 13th century this was probably the finest cathedral in Scotland and what remains of it is still impressive. The choir and the west front are particularly beautiful.

    Lossiemouth (10 km/6 ml) is a popular and well equipped centre on the Moray Firth with good beaches. *Aberdeen 106 km/66 ml; Braemar 109/68; Edinburgh 257/160; Inverness 60/38.*

Dunvegan Castle, Skye

EYEMOUTH (pop. 2200), *Berwick./ Borders* An attractive little fishing town once noted as a centre of smuggling. The area is one of cliffs and caves and good rock scenery. Pleasant places within easy reach are **Coldingham** (where the priory, founded in the 11th century, is one of the oldest churches still in use) which is now a major sub aqua centre: the quaint fishing village of **St Abbs**, and the village of **Burnmouth,** situated around a tiny harbour at the foot of a steep ravine by an often raging sea. *Berwick 16 km/10 ml; Edinburgh 77/48.*

FALKLAND (pop. 922), *Fife* This very attractive little town was once the centre of good hunting country, a fact which tempted the kings of Scotland to build a palace there. There is some delightful domestic architecture which contrasts strikingly with the lovely 16th-century palace. Make a point of seeing not only the interior, but the exterior—there is a very well planted garden and the Royal Tennis Court, still in use, dating from 1539. *Edinburgh 57 km/36 ml.*

FORT AUGUSTUS (pop. 887), *Inverness./Highland* A small village that owes its fame to the Benedictine abbey built in the 19th century on the ruins of the Duke of Cumberland's fort. Beside the canal in the village there is a museum which gives the history of the Great Glen and the history of the Loch Ness Monster. There have been many sightings from the abbey, over the centuries, of whatever it is in the loch. *Inverness 52 km/32½ ml.*

FORTINGALL *Perthshire/Tayside* See both the old thatched cottages and the ancient yew tree which is said to be somewhere between 2000 and 3000 years old. There are many archaeological sites in the vicinity of Fortingall, and there is a legend that Pontius Pilate was born there while his father was serving with a Roman legion. Certainly there are the remains of what appears to be a Roman Camp just south of the village. The river Lyon flows through **Glen Lyon** which runs west from Fortingall and is one of the loveliest glens in Scotland. To the south towers Ben Lawers (1325 m/3984 ft). If you do not have your own transport, enquire at Fortingall about the mail bus which can take the occasional passenger up to **Bridge of Balgie** post office, half way up the glen, and back. *Aberfeldy 13 km/8 ml.*

FORT WILLIAM (pop. 2851), *Inverness./Highland* One of the major touring centres of the West Highlands and focal point of the lovely Lochaber district, Fort William stands on Loch Linnhe, a long sea loch down which steamers sail for Oban and the Hebrides. The town offers excellent shops, sporting facilities and a reasonably easy route up **Ben Nevis** (1215 m/4406 ft). Tourists wishing to climb the ben should allow about six hours, and should not attempt it in bad weather or alone.

The small **Highland Museum,** which is situated in Cameron Square, contains a most interesting collection of Jacobite relics and should not be missed. If you are travelling by the A82 make a stop to see the Commando Memorial (18 km/11 ml NE of Fort William)— this was a training area for commandos in the Second World War. *Inverness 106 km/66 ml; Kyle of Lochalsh 111/69; Mallaig 72/45; Oban 79/49.*

FRASERBURGH (pop. 11,000), *Aberdeen./Grampian* Everything centres around the harbour here, for Fraserburgh is a fishing centre. If you like a bracing town with gulls wheeling around a busy harbour, Fraserburgh may be for you. It also offers an 18-hole golf course, a long sandy beach, 2 caravan sites, and has a lighthouse built atop the remains of a 16th-century tower. The other prominent historic building is the Wine Tower of about the same age. The original purpose of this puzzling tower is unknown, but possibly it was a lookout point. *Aberdeen 69 km/43 ml; Elgin 90/56; Montrose 129/80.*

GAIRLOCH (pop. 800), *Ross and Cromarty/Highland* This fishing village will appeal particularly to anglers and nature lovers, and nearby there are some fine beaches that are worth exploring. Travel to Gairloch by the road that runs along the side of Loch Maree, and you will see the kind of scenery that makes this district a favourite with motorists. By car you can visit

the villages of **Badachro** and **Flowerdale,** the exotic tropical gardens of **Inverewe** near Poolewe (National Trust property, open all the year round and worth a stop) and further north, on the road to Ullapool, the very lovely **Gruinard Bay,** approached by a steep descent. If you are travelling via **Kinlochewe,** stop at Aultroy Cottage, visitor centre for the Nature Conservancy (A832, NW of the village). You are on the doorstep here of the first national nature reserve in Britain, the **Beinn Eighe Reserve**—with a chance to meet the natural wonders often undreamed of by city dwellers. *Inverness 114 km/71 ml; Kyle of Lochalsh 111/69; Ullapool 92/57.*

GALASHIELS (pop. 12,300), *Selkirk/Borders* Ask a 'Gala' man which is the best town in the Borders and he will believe he is giving you an unbiased answer when he says Galashiels, for this is a town where loyalty runs high. It is not, in fact, the most attractive, especially as the approach from Edinburgh shows mill chimneys first. It is, however, a good centre for exploring the other towns and, indeed, has more charm than meets the eye. The 15th-century **Old Gala House** (now the Gala Arts Club) is one of the most endearing houses I have seen. Equally endearing is the town motto 'Sour Plums', which celebrates the murder of some English soldiers who were caught picking plums in the course of a border skirmish in 1337.

This is a bustling, expanding town, famed for its woollen and tweed manufacture, and the Scottish Woollen Technical College is situated here. There are several remains of ancient settlements in the area, notably **Rink Fort** with some impressive masonry. The local festival, the Braw Lads' Gathering, in which the Braw Lad and Lass ride with their retinue on a procession round the area, is held in early summer and commemorates the granting of a charter in 1599.

A pleasant excursion is to the beautifully situated village of **Stow** (8 km/5 ml) which has an ancient ruined church and a delightful 17th-century pack-horse bridge over the Gala Water. *Berwick 63 km/39 ml; Edinburgh 53/33; Glasgow 111/69; Peebles 31/19.*

GIFFORD *East Lothian/Lothian* A particularly pleasantly designed village set in the good rich farmlands of what was formerly East Lothian, it lies neatly around Yester House and probably many of the houses leading up to the impressive entrance gates once housed tenants of the estate. The 18th-century church is of particular interest to American visitors because a tablet there commemorates the birth at Gifford of the Rev. John Witherspoon (1723–94) who was one of the signatories of the American Declaration of Independence. He was also principal of Princeton University. *Haddington 6 km/4 ml.*

GIRVAN (pop. 6100), *Ayrshire/Strathclyde* Well down the Ayrshire coast, Girvan is a fishing port and boat building town as well as a popular resort. There is river and loch fishing, an excellent beach and good golf, tennis and bowling, but the town appeals most to those who love the sea. A popular sea trip is round the lonely rock of **Ailsa Craig**, teeming with seabirds. **Glenapp Castle** (A77,

24 km/15 ml SSW of Girvan) is worth visiting for its painted furniture and also for the gardens.

Turnberry Hotel and the two championship golf courses lie 8 km (5 ml) north of Girvan. *Ayr 34 km/21 ml; Glasgow 87/54; Largs 80/50.*

GLAMIS *Angus/Tayside* Two attractions here are the **Angus Folk Museum** at Kirkwynd Cottages and, of course, **Glamis Castle,** childhood home of the Queen Mother and presently the seat of the Earl and Countess of Strathmore. It is open to the public and worth seeing, as are the beautiful gardens. Nearby at **Kirriemuir,** is the birthplace, at 9 Brechin Road, of Sir J. M. Barrie (born 1860), where many of his personal possessions are exhibited. *Forfar 9 km/5½ ml.*

GLASGOW (pop. 900,000), *Lanark./Strathclyde* Edinburgh may be the most beautiful city in Scotland to choose as a base, but Glasgow, that great centre of international trade and industry, is certainly the most convenient. Because of its position on the very doorstep of the Clyde coast resorts and the soot-laden air of industrialization which hangs over the city, it has often been labelled 'the finest city in the world to get out of'.

This hardly does justice to Glasgow, for with half the country's population settled around it, the city can provide every entertainment for the visitor. Theatres, cinemas, sporting facilities, shops, 58 parks, museums are all there, at or near the city centre. For the first time in Scotland opera has a home of its own in the Theatre Royal (Hope Street) where **Scottish Opera**, a company acknowledged to be of the highest international standing, has its permanent base. Glasgow has an international reputation as a city of film-goers: as well as many central and suburban cinemas, there is the only purpose-built, full-time **Film Theatre** in Scotland, showing new and old films not often seen elsewhere (Rose Street). As well as containing the **Citizens' Theatre** (Gorbals Street, repertory) and the **King's** (Bath Street, touring companies) the city is the headquarters of **Scottish Ballet** and the **Scottish National Orchestra.** The Scottish Arts Council has an **Arts Centre** in Washington Street. The **Third Eye Centre** for art events and exhibitions, is in Sauchiehall Street.

There are fine examples of architecture, notably 'Greek' Thomson's sadly neglected church in **St Vincent Street,** and his **Caledonia Road Church** (1856–57), the absorbing **Glasgow School of Art** by Charles Rennie Mackintosh, brilliant exponent of Art Nouveau, and the **Cathedral,** the only virtually undamaged example of pre-Reformation Gothic architecture in Scotland. Although much of the building is 15th-century, the crypt is 12th-century and is one of the finest in the British Isles. Tradition says the tomb of St Mungo, who built a chapel on this site in the 6th century, is in the crypt. The 15th-century house **Provand's Lordship** (1471) is close to the Cathedral, and is probably the oldest house in Glasgow.

The **Art Gallery** at Kelvingrove (at the very west end of **Sauchiehall Street,** one of the main shopping streets) houses some magnificent paintings including Rembrandt's *A Man in Armour,* an excellent collection of French Impressionist and Post-Impressionist work, and Salvador Dali's *Christ of St John of the Cross.* Parts of Glasgow's famous Burrell Collection, a vast treasure of *objets d'art* of all kinds, now within sight of a permanent home, are displayed from time to time at Kelvingrove.

Enthusiasts of every age will enjoy the **Museum of Transport,** opened in 1964 at Eglinton Toll to house not only cars, bicycles and horse-drawn vehicles but a marvellous collection of tramcars from a horse-drawn tram of 1894 to a Coronation Tram of 1937. The **Children's Museum** at Tollcross Park has a good collection of dolls from all periods. Then there is the Zoo; the vast docks reaching into the centre of the city; the 19th-century **University Buildings** on University Avenue, a fine monument to the Victorian thirst for knowledge; and the complex of modern buildings above George Square which forms the nucleus of **Strathclyde University.** Glasgow is a good city to explore, and the friendly Glaswegians will help you to explore it, for they are proud of their city. The Scottish Tourist Board have a special leaflet that will ensure that you miss nothing. It is called *63 things to do in Glasgow.*

And yet, it is as a centre for seeing the Clyde coast and the west coast of Scotland generally that Glasgow is most loved. By bus, train or steamer you can go anywhere on the west coast. One of the most popular combined rail/steamer trips starts with a fast train to Craigendoran pier, where one joins the steamer bound for **Loch Goil** and **Loch Long.** At **Arrochar** 71 one disembarks, either to walk or take a bus the 3 km (2 ml) over to **Tarbet** on Loch Lomond. Another steamer sails past the beautiful islands of **Loch Lomond** to **Balloch** and the waiting train to Glasgow. This trip takes a whole day. In one long day you can get as far as **Oban** and the island of **Iona.** The information Bureau in George Square (*Tel.* 221-9600/7371) will provide information on all these tours and much else that Glasgow has to offer. *Callander 58 km/36 ml; Edinburgh 71/44; Largs 48/30; Perth 98/61.*

GLENCOE *Argyll./Highland*
Famous as the 'Glen of Weeping' and site of the massacre of the Clan Macdonald in 1692 because of its chieftain's supposed refusal to take an oath of allegiance to William III. He had, in fact, taken the oath, but bad weather and bureaucratic delays had caused him to be late in doing so. Campbell of Glen Lyon therefore carried out the king's instructions to kill the Macdonalds and raze their village. The overwhelming, brooding mountains bring the story of the massacre vividly to the minds of all who travel through it.

At the head of Glencoe is one of Scotland's three leading skiing centres, at which the most important championships take place. Ski tows and chairlifts at White Corries. Notable area for wildlife. In Glencoe village see the Bonnie Prince Charlie relics at the cottage museum. From the glen the road continues round the Black Mount and across the bleak **Moor of Rannoch,** again recalling *Kidnapped* and the escape of Alan Breck and David Balfour across this bog-ridden expanse. *Ballachulish 3 km/2 ml.*

GLENFINNAN *Inverness./ Highland* By road or rail it is also possible to visit this hamlet following the 'Road to the Isles' which lies on the scenic West Highland railway line to Mallaig. A quiet and lovely spot, on the shores of Loch Shiel, it is much visited because of the monument, inscribed in Gaelic, English and Latin, which marks the spot where Prince Charles Edward Stuart's standard was raised in 1745 to rally the clans to the Jacobite cause. The *Stage House Hotel* has excellent fishing rights. *Fort William 27 km/17 ml.*

GRANTOWN-ON-SPEY (pop. 1600), *Moray./Grampian* A pleasantly laid-out little town where tourism is the main occupation, Grantown is blessed with go-ahead hoteliers who have done much for this trade, especially in the organizing of the winter après-ski life of the town. During the skiing season there is some organized activity every evening of the week.

Fishing in the River Spey—one of the loveliest of Scottish rivers—is excellent and cheap. There is pleasant walking in the Strath Spey area, and for those with a car both sea and mountain scenery are within easy reach.

Grantown offers tennis, golf, bowling and annual sheep dog trials in summer, and in winter there is curling and skating in the town itself as well as highly organized skiing in the Cairngorms with instruction, equipment hire and transport facilities. *Edinburgh 225 km/140 ml; Elgin 53/33; Glasgow 248/154; Inverness 55/34.*

HADDINGTON (pop. 6672), *East Lothian/Lothian* A county town of high architectural interest, best seen on foot. It is said to be one of the best conserved towns in the country because it adheres to a large extent to its medieval street plan. Certainly there are few towns of this size that can boast that 129 of its buildings are scheduled as of Special Architectural or Historic Interest. There is a recommended walk around the town which takes in the main ones—the Town House designed by William Adam, Nungate Bridge, Poldrate Mill, the lovely St Mary's Parish Church (14th-century but recently renovated) and the buildings of the High Street. Haddington enjoys a considerable cultural life and there is usually some exhibition or event being organized that would interest the visitor. *Edinburgh 29 km/18 ml.*

HAWICK (pop. 16,000), *Roxburgh./ Borders* The largest of the Border towns, Hawick is the centre of the hosiery industry, producing knitwear for the fashion markets of the world. Not a particularly pretty town, it is an important centre in everyday life for the Borders, and has many tourist facilities. It has interesting historical associations, although virtually the whole town was burnt down in 1570, and nearby is **Hawick Mote**, believed to be the mound of a Norman castle. **Hawick Museum** is in Wilton Lodge Park on the outskirts of town and the park itself has pleasant riverside walks, gardens, etc.

There is a rumbustious local festival, the Hawick Common Riding, on the Friday and Saturday after the first Monday in June, when the elected Cornet and his retinue first inspect the town boundaries, and then continue

en fête into the second day. This is one of the best festivals for the tourist to see, and commemorates a victory over the English in 1514. The town song *Teribus ye Teri Odin* is said to be an invocation to the ancient gods, Thor and Odin. *Callander 164 km/102 ml; Carlisle 69/43; Edinburgh 82/51; Glasgow 134/83.*

INVERARAY (pop. 1000), *Argyll./ Strathclyde* The chief attraction of this little town, rebuilt on its present site in the 18th century, is the seat of the Duke of Argyll— **Inveraray Castle.** This most imposing building, at once a very early manifestation of the Gothic revival, yet with magnificent 18th-century interiors, had the top floor destroyed by fire in 1975 but is again open to the public, and is well worth a visit. Both the castle and the small town were built by the third Duke of Argyll, and many of the houses have since been modernized inside. The two, town and castle, form a complete unit, testament to an age of architectural graciousness. Ten km (6 ml) SSW of Inveraray on the A83 you will find **Auchindrain museum,** the nicest possible way of appreciating what life was like on a West Highland farm in the 18th century. Houses and farm buildings stand in their fields all furnished as in the period.

There are bus tours to Inveraray from Oban, and it can be reached by steamer from the Clyde, but beautifully placed near the head of Loch Fyne, it is also a pleasant centre from which to explore Argyll and the west coast. The woodland and garden at **Crarae** (16 km/10 ml SW of Inveraray) is open to the public. *Dunoon 77 km/ 48 ml; Glasgow 97/60; Oban 66/41.* 73

INVERNESS (pop. 30,500), *Inverness./Highland* If you are touring the Highlands by car and prefer to have a city base, Inverness is the ideal centre Even if you are without a car, Inverness, the most northerly large centre in Scotland and 'Capital of the Highlands', offers a comprehensive range of coach tours. As long ago as the 6th century it was capital of the Pictish kingdom and there are indications that its strategic position was appreciated long before then. The site of Macbeth's castle is 400 m ($\frac{1}{4}$ ml) east of the station. The museum and art gallery situated in Bridge Street contain interesting Jacobite relics.

The character of the town is that of a good shopping, distribution and social centre for the north. There are a large number of good quality small stores here as well as branches of national chain stores, and several antique shops; good tweeds and souvenirs are readily available. Although of ancient lineage, the appearance of Inverness is predominantly Victorian. This is mainly due to the imposing orange-red pink stone **Castle** with round towers, which stands so impressively above the River Ness. Do not be misled—this is not an ancient stronghold, although it stands on a site which has been in use since the 12th century, but an early Victorian building which houses the Sheriff Court and the Police Headquarters. Next to it is a modern shopping centre, looking grotesquely out of place.

The narrow streets of Inverness, which make traffic a great problem, are not attractive, but walk down to the river and the town takes on a gentler air. The river is spanned by several bridges, and on summer evenings there are often entertainments on the wooded islands about 1 km ($\frac{1}{4}$ ml) up river. In the first light of day you can stand on one of the bridges and watch a fisherman up to his waist in water casting for salmon in the Ness— and this in the centre of a large town spread over both banks.

Some of the prettiest houses are along the banks of the river, and many of these are guest houses and small hotels. On the west bank of the river stands **St Andrew's Episcopal Cathedral,** an attractive 19th-century building of pink stone surrounded by trees. If you are interested in ancient times take the Craig Phadraig forest walk on Leachkin Road (3 km/2 ml W of Inverness)— it leads to an Iron Age Pictish vitrified fort. *Edinburgh 254 km/ 158 ml; Elgin 61/38; Fort William 106/66; John o' Groats 212/132; Pitlochry 140/87.*

IONA (Inner Hebrides), *Argyll./ Western Isles* Iona, the Sacred Isle, is small and fairly flat. Its colouring is pale green and light grey, fringed here and there with blonde sand and turquoise sea. There are just two hotels, and a number of houses will take in guests. What does one do there? It depends on how long you are staying. Go on a day steamer trip from Oban, and you will have time for a brisk walk from the pier to the Abbey, and that is about all. It does not give you time to savour the atmosphere of this island where St Columba landed and founded a small monastery in AD 563 from which he undertook the conversion of Scotland and the north of England. A worthwhile trip is to **Staffa,** 11 km (7 ml) north, to see Fingal's

Cave with its basalt pillars.

Queen Margaret is said to have built **St Oran's Chapel** in the 11th century. In the next century came the **Abbey.** The present one was only recently restored by the Iona Community whose lay members worked on it every summer for many years. While the Community is in residence during August, the little isle sometimes seems ready to sink into the sea from sheer weight of numbers, but go in spring (May is a good month) to an interdenominational service at the Abbey, and you will see it at its quietest and best. Opposite the Abbey stands **St Martin's Cross,** over 5 m (16 ft) high, fine example of Celtic carving, and one of the two survivors of the 360 crosses that are said to have been on the island before the Reformation.

Iona is the burial place of 48 Scottish kings as well as rulers of France, Norway and Ireland, and indeed **St Oran's Cemetery** is the oldest Christian burial ground in Scotland. Walk to **Columba's Bay** at the south end—the island is only 5 km (3 ml) long—and scrabble around the pebble beach for Iona greenstone washed in by the tide. This is a pale green marble, and there is not a great deal of it. The colours of all the pebbles are fascinating, but wait until the green ones are dry and hold them up to the light, for only the translucent ones are genuine. These look most attractive set as jewellery.

On the west side of the island is the *machair,* a meadow of tiny wild flowers, which imperceptibly merges with sand to form a lovely beach and an excellent picnic spot. Iona is the perfect island for a peaceful vacation, yet there are good connections to Oban and to Fionphort on Mull, less than 1¼ km (1 ml) away. To stand on the shore in the failing light of evening and listen to the Abbey bells toll over the isle and the still sea is a memorable experience.

ISLAY and **JURA (Inner Hebrides),** *Argyll./Western Isles* Islay is a large island lying opposite the coast of Kintyre. Farming and distilling are the main activities, but in recent years tourism has become a profitable business. There is a daily air service from Glasgow, and a regular steamer service from West Loch Tarbert in Argyll (steamer connections to the Clyde). **Bowmore** is the capital, with **Port Ellen** and **Port Askaig** the other main centres. At **Kildalton** (12 km/7½ ml NE of Port Ellen) you will find in the churchyard two of the finest Celtic crosses in Scotland.

Cross by Feolin Ferry to the large but sparsely inhabited island of **Jura,** where the main settlement is at **Lagg,** and take the steamer to visit the nearby island of **Colonsay** with the sub-tropical gardens of Colonsay House. The Paps of Jura, three prominent mountains all around 760 m (2500 ft) high are the island's most remarkable feature. Separating Jura from the little island of **Scarba** to the north is the Strait of Corryvreckan with its famous whirlpool which can be heard from a long distance away.

JOHN O'GROATS See THURSO

KELSO (pop. 4922), *Roxburgh./ Borders* Probably the most important of the Border market towns, Kelso has a wide Georgian square reminiscent of French provincial towns in the area immediately around Paris. There are examples of attractive architecture in many old nooks of the town. Supreme in the area is **Floors Castle**, home of the Duke of Roxburgh. Floors, open to the public only one day a year (the last Sunday in August) was built by Vanbrugh in 1718 and has 365 windows, one for every day of the year. The ruins of **Kelso Abbey** give an impression of what the Border abbeys must have been like when they were at their wealthiest. They were, of course, the centres of learning from the 12th to at least the 16th century. From Kelso, the visitor should visit **Mellerstain House** (13 km/8 ml NW) one of the loveliest of the Adam 18th-century mansions. The lake and park, the terraced Italian garden, and the beautifully moulded ceilings and furnishings all make it worth seeing. There are many beautiful paintings, books and *objets d'art*.

The grounds of **The Hirsel,** home of Lord Home of the Hirsel, a former Prime Minister, are frequently open to the public (off the A697). *Edinburgh 83 km/52 ml.*

KILLIN (pop. 1265), *Perthshire/ Tayside* Killin at the west end of Loch Tay is very attractive because of the **Falls of Dochart** at the entrance to the village. The rock strewn bed of the river causes the water to froth and tumble and leap its way to the loch. The burial ground of the Clan MacNab is in Killin and the church (though itself only 18th-century) has a 9th-century font. It is not far from here to **Ben Lawers** on the north side of the loch. Take the A827 up to the National Trust Visitor

Centre (at 425 m/1400 ft) for ranger-guided walks, and information on botany and geology. *Aberfeldy 37 km/23 ml.*

KILMARNOCK (pop. 49,000), *Ayr./ Strathclyde* An inland industrial town which nevertheless is popular with those who like a town base, Kilmarnock has extensive parks, tennis, bowling, curling in winter, and two 18-hole golf courses. The first edition of Robert Burns' poems, the *Kilmarnock Edition,* was printed here in 1786, and in Kay Park stands the Burns Monument and Museum which contains manuscripts and relics.

Kilmarnock is within easy reach of the Ayrshire coast resorts of **Ardrossan, Saltcoats** and **Troon** —all served by the Clyde steamers —and Burns country. *Ayr 19 km/ 12 ml.*

KINGUSSIE See NEWTONMORE

KIRKCUDBRIGHT (pop. 3000), *Kirkcudbright./Dumfries and Galloway* Gracious Kirkcudbright (pronounced Kirkoo-brae) is a delightful little town, lying at the head of a bay into which flows the River Dee. There is a tiny harbour, many picturesque houses, and the *jougs* or iron collars, with which criminals, witches and such like were chained to a tolbooth or churchyard wall, can still be seen at the Mercat Cross (1610). The Tolbooth, where Paul Jones was imprisoned in 1778, and ruined McLellan's Castle date from the 16th century. Nowadays Kirkcudbright is a favourite haunt of artists, and many painters, weavers and potters live here. Art courses are held during the summer months, and there is always an exhibition of local work to be seen

in a cottage by the harbour.
Broughton House, once the home
of the artist E. A. Hornel, contains
many of his paintings, and is on
view to the public as is the small
but unusual garden.

A short distance west lies
Gatehouse of Fleet, another
attractive little place with
colour-washed cottages. Burns is
said to have written out the song
Scots wha Hae' in the *Murray Arms
Hotel,* now restored, modernized
and very comfortable. From
Gatehouse it is a pleasant walk
to old **Anwoth Church** (1 km/¾ ml)
which has a Dark Age cross in the
churchyard. Another pleasant walk
is to the beach at **Sandgreen** where
there is a caravan (trailer) park
or to 15th-century **Cardoness
Castle** (1½ km/1 ml SW of
Gatehouse) where the elaborate
fireplaces are such a feature.
*Dumfries 43 km/27 ml; Edinburgh
161/100; Hawick 129/80; Perth
232/144.*

KYLE OF LOCHALSH (pop. 400),
Ross and Cromarty/Highland The
village itself has nothing much to
offer but it lies in a choice
situation on the west coast directly
opposite Skye, and offers
magnificent views of the island.
The Kyleakin–Kyle of Lochalsh
car ferry takes only a few minutes
to make the crossing, so narrow
is the strait that divides Skye from
the mainland at this point. The
pier is always a centre of interest,
for boats call here connecting with
Mallaig, Armadale, Portree (on
Skye), Stornoway (on Lewis), and
the Outer Hebrides.

Although Kyle is primarily the
gateway to Skye, it can be used as
a base for touring a lovely area.
It is the terminus of the railway
line from Inverness, a lovely

journey up Glen Carron, via
Achnasheen, Garve and Dingwall.
In the other direction, one can
drive down to Dornie and the
restored and exceptionally
photogenic **Eilean Donan Castle**
standing on an island in Loch
Duich, reached from the shore by
an old stone causeway. From any
road in this area one gets a
magnificent view of striking
mountains called the **Five Sisters
of Kintail** (the highest is 1070 m/
3505 ft) which run south-east from
Loch Duich. *Carlisle 428 km/266 ml;
Edinburgh 325/202; Glasgow 277/
172; Ullapool 140/87.*

LAIRG (pop. 1000), *Sutherland/
Highland* There is nothing
especially beautiful about Lairg,
and its main importance is as the
railhead for the north of Scotland.
A glance at the map on page 49 will
show that Lairg is also at the heart
of the northern road network. Bus
services radiate to Ullapool,
Lochinver and Durness, and it
makes an excellent touring centre.
Amongst other amenities, it has
one particularly good hotel, the
Sutherland Arms. Lairg is also an
excellent fishing centre. *Dingwall
61 km/38 ml; Edinburgh 338/210;
Glasgow 346/215; Inverness 84/52;
John o' Groats 143/89.*

LARGS (pop. 10,000), *Ayr./
Strathclyde* Largs is an immensely
popular and well equipped seaside
resort, catering especially well for
children with traditional
amusements. There are very
sheltered waters for sailing, and the
Royal Largs Yacht Club holds two
regattas in the summer season.
There are also facilities for golf,
fishing, tennis and bowling. Just
behind the Main Street is
Skelmorlie Aisle, the impressive

mausoleum of the 17th-century Parish Church of St Columba. South of Largs stands a slim tower which commemorates the Battle of Largs (1263).

There are pleasure cruises and steamer connections with Rothesay and all the other Clyde resorts as well as with **Millport**—equally popular—on the island of Great Cumbrae opposite. *Ardrossan 19 km/12 ml; Callander 101/63; Glasgow 48/30.*

LEWIS (pop. 24,000) and **HARRIS** (pop. 3200), *Western Isles* The Outer Hebrides are basically one long stretch of land cut by the sea into three portions of which Lewis and Harris form the most northerly portion. Although officially two islands, and distinctly different in scenery—Lewis is generally flat, Harris hilly and dominated by Clisham (796 m/2622 ft)—they are in fact one, divided by the old county border near Loch Seaforth where the Seaforth Highlanders regiment was raised.

Lewis is not attractive, although there are fine beaches and cliff scenery, particularly at **Uig,** but it does have **Stornoway,** the capital of the Outer Isles, a proper town and, indeed, the only one on the islands. With a population of 5400, Stornoway is a fair size with a good and busy harbour, an airport with regular services to the mainland, daily steamers from Mallaig and Kyle of Lochalsh. There is a wool mill to provide alternative industry to the traditional fishing. **Stornoway Castle** is now a technical college, but the grounds (with an 18-hole golf course) are open to the public. Stornoway may be far from the mainland, but there is no lack of life. Saturday in Cromwell Street when the

islanders come to do their weekly shopping will make you feel you are anything but far from the centre of things.

At **Shawbost** (30 km/19 ml NW of Stornoway) there is a museum and mill—together they illustrate the old way of life in Lewis. From Stornoway one sight you should try to see is the Standing Stones of **Callanish** (24 km/15 ml), second in importance only to Stonehenge and just as mysterious. The tallest stone is almost 6 m (18 ft) high, and there are 47 of them. Who put them there, how and why, no one is likely to know, but they have stood on this bleak, windswept island for perhaps 3000 years, and they give an extremely eerie feeling. At **Arnol** (24 km/15 ml NW of Stornoway) there is a 'black house', the old type of dwelling of the Hebrides, so-called because there was no chimney and the smoke from the peat fire blackened the interior walls.

The easiest way of travelling south to **Harris** is to take the regular bus from Stornoway which drops mail, milk, boxes of newborn chickens and passengers all along its way. Travelling by bus is one of the delights of the Outer Hebrides. Make for **Tarbert,** a pretty village and a good centre. It should be possible to visit the nearby isle of **Scalpay,** an attractive little place. A mail boat makes regular calls, and this makes an interesting trip, which gives you a good idea of the way of life of the islanders.

The bus continues right round Harris to **Rodel** (37 km/23 ml) on the southern tip where it stops long enough for you to look at the 15th-century Church of St Clement. This is well worth a visit: the situation is perfect, the building is in complete harmony with the peaceful surroundings, and the inscriptions on the gravestones are fascinating. The bus route continues via **Leverburgh** and magnificent deserted sandy beaches back to Tarbert. This island is famous, of course, for Harris Tweed, and the local tourist association may be able to introduce you to a weaver, who will show you how it is made and perhaps sell you a length of tweed. *From Stornoway: Rodel 92 km/57 ml; Tarbert 55/34; Uig 40/25.*

LINLITHGOW (pop. 5191), *West Lothian/Lothian* In itself, Linlithgow is not a particularly attractive town except for the loch with the ancient palace at one end. Though it was burned down in 1746, the remains are substantial enough to give a feeling of its earlier splendour. St Michael's church nearby is medieval but it wears a modern golden crown— a piece of restoration that caused much controversy when it was done a few years ago. Those who like a slow pace to their travels, should ask locally about cruises on the Linlithgow Union Canal. These are planned to be by a horse-drawn barge called *The Queen of the Union.*

Six km (4 ml) east of the town, there is a stately home which belongs to the National Trust but has been the home of the Dalyells for centuries. If you go on a Saturday afternoon you may take a guided walk of the nature trail in the parkland. Going in the other direction you come to **Kinneil House** (off A904) where, in an outhouse, James Watt developed the steam engine. Or take the road to **South Queensferry** and see the grandest house of them all, home of the Marquess of Linlithgow. **Hopetoun House** was designed first by Sir William Bruce in the 17th century then added to by the Adams. It contains great treasures, especially in pictures by Rubens, Rembrandt and Canaletto. There are deer in the parkland, St Kilda sheep and beautiful birds. *Edinburgh 28 km/17½ ml; Glasgow 48/30.*

LOCHEARNHEAD (pop. 300), *Perth./Tayside* Lochearnhead is noted as the home of the first Northern European Water Skiing Championships in Scotland, organized by an enterprising hotel owner there in 1966. The village stands at the east end of Loch Earn amidst lovely scenery. However, **St Fillans**, the village at the east end offering golf, fishing and boating, is even lovelier. One can climb Ben Vorlich (982 m/3224 ft) from here, and there is good accommodation at both ends of the loch. Indeed, these two villages are ideal for a few days in peaceful and very beautiful surroundings.

A particularly pleasant day trip is round the triangle created by Lochearnhead, Pitlochry and Perth, passing through **Killin,** a short distance north of Lochearnhead at the west end of Loch Tay. Not far along Loch Tayside from Killin one passes Ben Lawers (1214 m/3984 ft) where a great variety of Apline plants grow wild. Visitors are requested not to pick these flowers which are of great interest to botanists. *Glasgow 85 km/53 ml; Oban 95/59; Perth 58/36; Pitlochry 76/47.*

LOCHINVER (pop. 200), *Sutherland/Highland* Perhaps my favourite of all the north-western fishing villages, Lochinver is also one of the most remote. There is not a great deal of tourist accommodation, but if you can book ahead, it is worth spending a few days there. The village lies in a bay with a little bridge at either end spanning two rushing, gushing streams. In between is one street of little houses and a few shops, and in early spring you will meet more sheep walking along the street than people.

What can you do there? Fish, birdwatch, mountaineer—Suilven (730 m/2399 ft), Canisp, Cul More and Stac Polly rise up suddenly from relatively flat stretches of bleak moorland, giving a weird lunar aspect to the area. You can watch the unloading and sale of the catch when the little fishing fleet comes into the harbour below the hotel. You can hire a car to take you to Ullapool (61 km/38 ml) if it rains, and above all you can walk amidst some of the loveliest scenery in Scotland. There is water everywhere—around 280 named lochs in this one parish; every bend of the road shows another lochan, and tucked into every corner is a cottage with a breathtaking view. The local people are extremely friendly and have a healthy curiosity about any visitor.

There is a bus service from Lairg (74 km/46 ml). If, however, you have your own transportation, use it to explore the north coast via Kylesku Ferry, the village of **Scourie** (48 km/39 ml) with the most northerly palm trees in the world, and up to **Durness** (89 km/55 ml). There are two hotels up here; the *Cape Wrath*, and a small one near the Smoo Cave, a great rocky cavern on the beach which was once used by smugglers. At **Balnakeil** (1 km/½ ml W of Durness)

there is a craft village which is worth visiting to see the craftsmen at work, and, of course, to buy well made souvenirs. The road continues east to **Tongue** (150 km/93 ml), where there is good bathing and fishing, although the shores of the north are very exposed and one is reminded that there is nothing to break the wind as it sweeps down from Greenland. All along this road one is continually catching sight of Ben Loyal, a handsomely shaped mountain of 763 m (2504 ft). *Inverness 174 km/108 ml.*

MALLAIG (pop. 600), *Inverness./Highland* Although not a beautiful village itself, Mallaig is an important centre for the tourist because it stands at the head of the beautiful West Highland line from Fort William, and is also one of the main ports of call for steamers to both the Inner and Outer Hebrides. It is a big fishing centre with a deep-freeze unit and lobster pond.

If you prefer a quieter spot, both **Arisaig** and **Morar** are a short distance south. This area is associated with Bonnie Prince Charlie, for it was around here that he landed from Europe to lead the Jacobite rising of 1745, and after its failure, it was again from this district that a ship took him back to France.

There is excellent sea, loch and river fishing at Morar (Loch and River Morar), and the white sands that run along this part of the coast to Arisaig are famous. *Glasgow 243 km/151 ml; Inverness 175/109; Ullapool 175/109.*

MELROSE (pop. 2000), *Roxburgh./Borders* A quiet Border town which is worth visiting primarily because

80

of the remains of its lovely **Abbey,** founded by David I, where Robert the Bruce's heart is said to have been buried after its return from Spain. A surprising amount of this building stands, mainly of 15th-century origin. There are some excellent bits of statuary still recognizable on the outside walls, and outstandingly beautiful tracery work, particularly on the window in the south transept. (Department of Environment property.)

This little town consists of a few streets radiating from the square where there is an attractive Mercat Cross (1642). It has several hotels, two antique shops and at The Penstead, off the main street, the work of two popular local artists is on view to the public. It is a pleasant centre for a few quiet days and a good base from which to visit **Abbotsford** (5 km/3 ml), Sir Walter Scott's stately home, still much as it was in his day (he died there in 1832), the Abbeys of **Dryburgh** (where Scott is buried), **Jedburgh** with its magnificent nave, and **Kelso** which, like all the Border abbeys, has been largely destroyed by the English and subsequent plunderers who made use of the masonry for other buildings. *Carlisle 95 km/59 ml; Edinburgh 61/38; Glasgow 108/67.*

MILLPORT *Bute/Strathclyde* This is the only town on the island of Cumbrae, one of the scattering of Firth of Clyde islands. Going by car ferry from Largs (connected by rail with Glasgow), the crossing takes about ten minutes. Millport is a popular little resort with that attractive feeling of having its own special identity that comes only with island life. There is just one road round the island and bicycles (which can be hired in Millport)

are the best means of seeing everything.

MONTROSE (pop. 10,000), *Angus/ Tayside* One of the attractive east coast family resorts, Montrose boasts 6 km (4 ml) of magnificent sands, two 18-hole golf courses and many other sporting facilities including a large indoor swimming pool. Some yachting is possible in the large tidal basin behind the town, but when the tide is out this is a favourite spot with naturalists, for large numbers of birds congregate there. It is a lively little town with many attractive old houses, a broad High Street, and an elegant 18th-century **Town Hall,** for this was a fashionable Scottish spa in the 18th century. Little closes reach back from the High Street to tempt photographers. **Edzell Castle,** itself a ruin, still has a beautiful walled garden, created in 1604, frequently illustrated in glossy gardening books. The castle is off the B996 about 10 km (6 ml) north of Brechin. *Aberdeen 60 km/37 ml; Braemar 101/63; Edinburgh 132/82; Perth 77/48.*

MULL (pop. 1700), *Argyll./ Western Isles* A big island about 40 km by 32 km (25 ml by 20 ml), largely given to majestic mountains. If you do not want to stay there, you can see a good part of the island by travelling this way to Iona: boat (passenger and car ferry) from Oban to **Craignure** on Mull where buses meet the boats. There is a large modern hotel in Craignure. The bus crosses to the other side of the island through the vast, almost deserted **Glen Moire** and along the coast of **Loch Scridain** to the settlement of **Fionphort** on the western side and the little ferry to Iona. In fine weather it makes a very pleasant trip, but on overcast days, when the mist is rolling down Mull's mountains, the atmosphere can become rather dreich and scary.

The main town on Mull is **Tobermory** (pop. 750). Approaching it on the steamer from Oban (thrice weekly) or Lochaline, it is as trim and fresh looking a haven as you could wish to see and it has one of the safest anchorages in the Western Isles. The largest hotel, *The Western Isles,* is in an enviable position on a high rocky headland overlooking the harbour. There is usually something happening in the town in the way of entertainment, and walking and golfing (9-hole course) are favourite pursuits. Mail boats are the best way of exploring the area: one goes to **Ardnamurchan Point** on the mainland, and there is a little hotel at **Kilchoan** not far away where you may well have time for lunch or a drink before the mail boat makes its way back to Tobermory.

A passable road touches small villages round the coast of Mull (bus services), and there are several small beaches. Another village which provides for a quiet holiday in much the same style is **Salen** which is connected by bus to Tobermory.

On the west coast the most attractive village is **Dervaig.** There are pleasant coastal walks here and entertainment of a unique sort in Mull's Little Theatre which has seating for only a few people and specializes in plays for casts of two players.

NAIRN (pop. 8000), *Nairn./ Highland* This small town is an outstanding family resort with wonderful beaches along the Moray Firth whose great breakers crash on the sand on stormy days. Nairn offers excellent fishing, three golf courses (two 18-hole), and a golfing week in May. A large green runs down to the beach, and the beautiful sands are extensive. Beside the small harbour there is a large caravan site where caravans may be hired by the week.

Nearby are **Cawdor Castle** (18 km/11 ml), a magnificent medieval fortress with a central tower built in 1454 and surrounded by lovely gardens: and the site of the **Battle of Culloden,** marked by a great cairn beside B9006, where the forces of the Duke of Cumberland defeated Prince Charles Edward Stuart and his 5000 Highlanders in 1746. *Aberdeen 142 km/88 ml; Braemar 118/70; Inverness 25/16; Kyle of Lochalsh 156/97.*

NEW LANARK *Lanark./ Strathclyde* You must go first to the busy market town of **Lanark** then find the road that slips down to the river's edge. Here is New Lanark, founded in the late 18th century by Dale and Arkwright in an effort to give decent housing to those finding employment in the mills that were the product of the Industrial Revolution. The name best remembered from the brave experiment is that of Robert Owen (1771–1858), a man who tried to care for the workers when so many merely used them. There have been plans for the restoration of the village but these go at a slow pace due to lack of funds. *Lanark 2 km/ 1 ml.*

NEWTONMORE (pop. 2100) and **KINGUSSIE** (pop. 1100), *Inverness./ Highland* Both popular Speyside villages geared to summer and winter tourism. Newtonmore offers skiing in the Cairngorms, curling, fishing and good walking as well as golf, tennis, pony trekking and a clan museum (Clan Macpherson). Newtonmore is where pony trekking was 'invented' as a sport, and it is still one of the major centres for it.

Eight km (5 ml) west is **Kingussie** which offers the same sporting facilities. Parents and children acquire painlessly a little of the social history of Scotland by visiting the **Am Fasgadh Museum** which has a fascinating collection of Highland antiquities—furniture, domestic utensils, dresses—of the last 200 years as well as a furnished cottage, a mill from Lewis and a 'black house', etc. *Inverness 74 km/46 ml; Perth 114/71; Mallaig 148/92.*

NEWTON STEWART (pop. 1965), *Wigtown./Dumfries and Galloway*

A pleasant town on the River Cree —a good holiday and fishing centre—lying on the edge of **Glen Trool Forest Park**. At **Creetown** (10 km/6 ml SE of Newton Stewart) there is a gem/rock museum with exhibits from all over the world. *Stranraer 37 km/23½ ml.*

NORTH BERWICK (pop. 4000), *East Lothian/Lothian*

From Berwick Law, a conical, grassy and volcanic hill over 180 m (600 ft) high, one gets a magnificent view of the countryside around this popular resort. One can see a large stretch of the Forth with its little islands, one of which, the **Bass Rock,** is the home of hundreds of screeching gannets (boat trips around the Bass are a popular outing). To the south stretch the rich farming lands of East Lothian. Nearer hand are the **Lodge Grounds,** extensive parkland open to the public, and along the coast the extremely interesting 14th-century ruins of rose-coloured **Tantallon Castle** (5 km/3 ml). Golf is the main attraction (two 18-hole, one 9-hole), but there are also good shops, a harbour mainly used by pleasure boats, a fine open air swimming pool, and a full programme of traditional seaside events.

There are excellent hotels, the most expensive ones being near the celebrated golf course. Almost every second house offers accommodation in the season.

There are several attractive villages in the area. **Gullane,** famous for its golf courses which include the championship course of Muirfield; **Aberlady**—its bay is a nature reserve, and there is a collection of cars at the Myreton Motor Museum here; **Dirleton**— an interesting ruined castle stands on one side of the green in this delightful village. *Edinburgh 39 km/ 24 ml; Glasgow 108/67; St Andrews 117/73; Stirling 97/60.*

NORTH UIST, BENBECULA, SOUTH UIST (pop. ca. 7000), *Inverness./Western Isles*

These islands form the central portion of the Outer Isles. Car ferries connect Lochmaddy (North Uist) and Lochboisdale (South Uist) with Mallaig, and the plane to Stornoway makes a stop at Benbecula. A bus runs all the way from Lochmaddy (boat connections to Tarbert, Harris) to Lochboisdale, crossing the Atlantic on causeways between North Uist and Benbecula, and Benbecula and South Uist.

Lochmaddy and **Lochboisdale** are both centres for those who seek the quiet life with some fishing. Both North and South Uist have good brown and sea trout fishing and North Uist also offers salmon fishing.

On a piece of high ground to the north of South Uist, a Catholic island, stands a beautiful statue 9 m (30 ft) in height. Called 'Our Lady of the Isles', by the sculptor Hew Lorimer, it portrays the Virgin and child. It makes a most moving and majestic landmark, visible from far out to sea. *Lochmaddy to Lochboisdale 92 km/45 ml.*

OBAN (pop. 7000), *Argyll./ Strathclyde* Never dull, never garish, Oban is an unparalleled base for those who wish to tour, sail or just stay put. It is best seen from the sea, from a boat coming in from the quiet Hebrides, for then the lively bustling air of the town strikes fresh. The contrasting colours of sea, hills and township exemplify the particular beauty of the Western Highlands, and **MacCaig's Tower** or **Folly** rises above the town to tease the mind of the visitor. This was built by an Oban man to give work to his fellow townsmen during a depressed period of the 19th century, and was intended as a family memorial and museum: but he died before its completion, and the tower remains in its unfinished state, a distinctive landmark.

There is a wide range of accommodation available with forty-odd hotels on the sea front alone, two golf courses, tennis courts, bowling greens, fishing, yachting and bathing. **Ganavan Sands** lie 3 km (2 ml) north of the town, linked by a regular bus service, and there is a large caravan site there. Shopping is excellent. In particular there are fine tweeds in subdued, misty Scottish colouring. One shop which attracts so many visitors that it is one of Oban's major attractions is the 'Gem Box'. Here, each window is given to a different semi-precious stone, mounted in a variety of settings—windowfuls of soft, pink rose-quartz and deep blue chalcedony.

Oban Bay is sheltered by the island of **Kerrera** which is 6 km (4 ml) long and mainly given over to agriculture. If you want to visit the ruined **Gylen Castle** on the island, a ferry leaves from Gallanach Road. For longer steamer trips, enquire at the Caledonian MacBrayne office at the pier. Boats for the Inner and Outer Hebrides leave regularly, and there is also a varied list of pleasure cruises of which the most popular is to Iona. Service buses cover the surrounding countryside, and there is a wide variety of bus tours, from those taking a few hours to nearby beauty spots, to full scale tours covering the great sights of the Highlands and Islands. Gardeners will be interested in the cherries and azaleas of the gardens at An Cala at **Easdale** (24 km/15 ml SW of Oban).

One particularly beautiful drive from Oban is the trip round Loch Awe, one of Scotland's loveliest lochs (some 113 km/70 ml). The loch is 40 km (25½ ml) long and 1 km (¾ ml) wide at its broadest point, its banks are tree-clad and its waters studded with islands. **Kilchurn Castle** at the north-east end of Loch Awe is one of the finest baronial ruins in the Western Highlands. **Killanure Church,** near the village of Ford at the southern end of the loch, was mentioned in the Argyll Charters of 1394, and is said to be haunted. If travelling on the A85 stop at the Cruachan Power Station visitors' centre (24 km/15 ml E of Oban). There are guided tours—well worth doing since the station is built inside the mountain of Ben Cruachan. *Edinburgh 198 km/123 ml; Glasgow 150/93; Mallaig 156/97; Pitlochry 148/92.*

ORKNEY and SHETLAND are
both large complexes of small islands scattered across the North Sea, Orkney consisting of some 70 islands and Shetland of 100, although the vast majority are uninhabited. For the lover of outdoor activities and quiet relaxing vacations, these islands have a special appeal, enhanced by the long summer days when, even at midnight, it is no darker than twilight and the countryside shimmers in the extraordinary 'Simmer dim' light.

The Orkneys lie only 32 km (20 ml) off the mainland. From Wick to Kirkwall, the capital, takes only half an hour by air, or you can take the mail boat from Thurso which will land you at Stromness, the second town of the islands. **Kirkwall** (pop. 4500), has narrow flagstoned streets, full of interesting architecture, and a beautiful 12th-century Cathedral, St Magnus, which mercifully remained untouched through the period of the Reformation although it was desecrated by Cromwell's soldiers. It is a lively base for tourists, for it is a good shopping centre and the starting point of bus and boat tours. Don't miss Earl Patrick's Palace which is said to be the most accomplished piece of Renaissance architecture left in Scotland (built 1607), and also the nearby Bishop's Palace (13th-century). Tankerness House in Broad Street, Kirkwall, which was formerly a merchant laird's mansion is now a museum to Orkney life.

Stromness (pop. 1600), has a good golf course and excellent beaches. It faces the island of **Hoy** (pop. 700), the second island of the Orkneys, where the Old Man of Hoy—a striking 137 m (450 ft) stack of red sandstone—typifies the stark, natural beauty of the windswept isles. Off the B9059, 2 km (1½ ml) NE of **Dounby** you can see Click Mill, the only working example of a horizontal water mill in Orkney. Perhaps the biggest attraction in Orkney is **Skara Brae,** a 4000 year old village, once covered by sand which was swept away in a storm of the last century to reveal the kind of Stone Age village archaeologists dream about. At **Birsay** are the absorbing 16th-century ruins of Birsay Palace. These northern islands are perfect for children; and the naturalist has endless wildlife to observe. At St Margaret's Hope, **Lamb Holm,** there is a chapel built by Italian prisoners of war (in 1943). They used tin cans to make the ironwork and did much remarkable hand painting.

In the 96 km (60 ml) between Orkney and Shetland lie **Foula** and **Fair Isle,** both inhabited, the latter being the home of a distinctive type of hand knitwear made by the local women. Although there are no patterns as such, the knitter 'making it up as she goes along', there are two basic types of pattern. The Fair Isle pattern takes the form of a wide band of colour at the neck or bottom of the garment; the Norwegian pattern uses colour over the whole garment and breaks down into panels. Sleeves are grafted rather than sewn on. Both of these islands have populations of rather less than 50 inhabitants and are not always easy to reach (mail boat service from Shetland in summer).

Shetland, too, has produced a distinctive type of knitting seen to advantage in the exquisite Shetland shawls which, though large enough to swaddle a baby, are so fine that they can be drawn through a wedding ring. The main towns are the capital, **Lerwick** (pop. 6000), an important centre of the fishing industry and, since Shetland's entry on the scene of North Sea oil, a very busy centre, and **Scalloway.** Lerwick has a quaint, bustling air, some of its houses have their foundations literally in the sea, and it is a natural touring base. It is the ancient capital of the islands, and is overshadowed by the 16th-century ruins of Scalloway Castle. Shetland has several sites of archaeological interest—none as old as Orkney's—of which **Jarlshof,** reckoned to be 2600 years old, shows signs of many and differing periods of occupation.

Both Orkney (brown trout) and Shetland (sea trout) offer excellent fishing. In some places it is free, in others a day's fine fishing will be inexpensive. In both groups visitors will be struck by the strong Scandinavian elements in the people who speak of 'Scotland' in the same way as England or France. The islands only became part of Scotland in the 15th century, and the Norse influence has remained and is kept alive by the fact that Lerwick is an important base for Norwegian fishermen, some of whom marry Shetland girls. The islands lie, of course, closer to Bergen than they do to Edinburgh, and the language is spattered with old Norse words.

There are regular shipping services from Aberdeen and Scrabster (Caithness) to Lerwick, and there are also services between the two groups. Air services connect Glasgow and Aberdeen with Shetland where the airport is at Sumburgh, near Jarlshof on the southern tip of the main island (Lerwick 42 km/26 ml).

Though **Sullom Voe** (40 km/25 ml N of Lerwick) could hardly be described as a tourist attraction (a voe is a narrow bay) this area is important as a North Sea oil pipeline terminal and tanker port—likely eventually to be Britain's biggest oil centre.

PEEBLES (pop. 6000), *Peebles./ Borders* A county town with a relaxed, friendly feeling about it. Peebles has good shops, a large Hydro Hotel, facilities for fishing, golf (18-hole), pony trekking, and many historical associations. Royal hunting parties came here— its former castle was a favourite hunting lodge of Alexander III— and it has been a royal burgh since the 14th century. It stands on the River Tweed, one of Scotland's great fishing rivers, which is spanned by an attractive 15th-century bridge, and is the centre of lovely walking country, wooded, green and hilly. Many famous men have connections with Peebles— Mungo Park, the African explorer; Sir Walter Scott (the *Cross Keys Hotel* is said to be Scott's Cleikum Inn in *St Ronan's Well*); and John Buchan. There is an interesting museum in the Chambers Institute which incorporates part of the 17th-century Queensberry Lodging. Nearby (2 km/1¼ ml) is **Neidpath**

Castle on the banks of the Tweed with massive 3 m (11 ft) walls. Excellent camping, caravanning and picnic site at **Rosetta Park.** Those interested in trees should try to see **Dawyck Gardens** (on B712 13 km/8 ml SW of Peebles) where there are many rare specimens, as well as magnificent rhododendrons.

The local festival, the Beltane Festival, is held on the last Saturday in June and is a typical example of the Border Riding festivals.

While in the area it is worth detouring to **Biggar** (A702, 21 km/13 ml W of Peebles) to see the Gladston Court street museum. Ask at the local ironmongers shop in the main street about it, since the premises and the inspiration were theirs. The museum is in the form of a Victorian street of shops set up with authentic stock. This is just one of the museum projects Biggar is planning; the project to have an open air folk museum is also developing.

Traquair House (13 km/8 ml E of Peebles) goes back to the 10th century, and should not be missed. It is the oldest continuously inhabited house in the country, and is full of fascinating exhibits. *Callander 119 km/74 ml; Edinburgh 37/23; Glasgow 80/50; Jedburgh 56/35.*

PERTH (pop. 43,000), *Perth./ Tayside* Perth is often referred to as the 'Fair City', but approach it from the south and you will wonder why, for your eyes will fall first on a tiny harbour, a grim prison, and a large rail complex. Once in the town, however, you will find charm in buildings such as the crown-turreted church **St Leonard's in the Field** which faces one of the two Inches—open parks by the banks of the River Tay; the magnificent 15th-century **Church of St John** off South Street; the **Fair Maid of Perth's House** off Charlotte Street; and in streets like **Rose Terrace** by the North Inch with its gracious Georgian houses. But go first to the visitor centre in **Marshall Place** to see the slide show and to make sure you are missing nothing of special interest to you.

Perth has strong claims as the first capital of Scotland—indeed, it was until the middle of the 15th century. **Scone Palace,** in whose grounds horse racing is now held, was once the crowning place of Scottish kings upon the celebrated Stone of Scone which was brought there from Dunstaffnage Castle in Argyll by Kenneth Macalpine, King of the Picts and Scots, in AD 843 to be used as the coronation stone. Tradition has it that this is the stone Jacob used as a pillow by Bethel. Edward I took it to Westminster Abbey where it now lies, but the last king to be crowned at Scone was Charles II in 1651.

Every keen gardener should try to see **Branklyn Gardens** on the Dundee Road, just outside Perth, especially for the fine collection of meconopsis which they feature.

For the rest, Perth is a busy market town with a lively repertory theatre, an art gallery and museum, and facilities for golf, fishing, tennis, bowls and boating. There are many shops of good quality serving a wealthy community, and it is a good centre for buying antiques. The annual bull sales in February are an international event, buyers from all over the world, particularly North and South America, converge on the town. Those interested in militaria should see **Balhousie Castle** in Hay Street for its exhibition of the history of the Black Watch regiment. If you are travelling north on the A93 watch out for the highest beech hedge in the world—planted in 1746 and now 26 m (85 ft) high. *Braemar 79 km/49 ml; Edinburgh 71/44; Fort William 166/103; Montrose 77/48.*

PETERHEAD (pop. 14,000), *Aberdeen./Grampian* Peterhead is known to Scots as a fishing centre and the home of a prison. Even the tourist cannot escape knowing these two facts about this red granite town, for fishing and fish processing are still major industries, and everything revolves around the National Harbour of Refuge whose great breakwater was built by convicts from the nearby prison. Nevertheless, Peterhead has some fine sandy beaches to the north of the town and 14 km (9 ml) to the south is **Cruden Bay** with 3 km (2 ml) of excellent clean, hard sand. There is also fine rock scenery to the south, there are a couple of ruined castles (**Inverugie**, 5 km/3 ml, and **Ravenscraig**, 2 km/1 ml), two golf courses (one 18-hole), fishing and, above all, the kind of healthy bracing air one would expect from the most easterly town in Scotland. Also worth seeing are Arbuthnott Church (dating from 13th century) and Arbuthnott museum and art gallery for its whaling exhibits. Between Peterhead and Aberdeen there is much pleasant coastal scenery— try the tiny resort of **Collieston** for the sheer accessibility of the sea, the main element of this area.

88   *Aberdeen 55 km/34 ml; Edinburgh 234/151; Elgin 95/59.*

PITLOCHRY (pop. 3000), *Perth./Tayside* Pitlochry is beautifully situated in the Tummel Valley and makes an exceptionally fine walking and touring centre, for this is a particularly lovely part of Scotland at all seasons. Apart from fishing, golf (18-hole), tennis, pony trekking and bowling and a few excellent shops, Pitlochry's main attractions are Faskally Dam and the Festival Theatre. The Tummel Hydro-Electric Scheme involved the damming of the Tummel which created Loch Faskally, now a local beauty spot, and at the **Faskally Dam**—a few minutes' walk from the centre of town—there is a fish ladder with an observation chamber where visitors can watch the salmon as they swim up the river to the spawning grounds. Here, the best months are July and August.

The **Pitlochry Festival Theatre** presents a repertory of 5 plays from May to October. The programme is well chosen, varied and always enjoyable. Meals and snacks are served in the foyer of the theatre which is also used for art exhibitions. Pitlochry first nights have become established social events in Scotland, and accommodation is severely taxed on these occasions, but it has an excellent range of accommodation from a large Hydro and first class hotels run by families, to bed and breakfast apartments. There are good caravan sites. *Aberdeen 150 km/92 ml; Braemar 64/40; Kyle of Lochalsh 219/136; Perth 43/27.*

PLOCKTON *Ross and Cromarty/Highland* Possibly the most beautiful village in Scotland, Plockton is only 8 km (5 ml) from

Kyle of Lochalsh. With only one hotel, it is in no danger of becoming tourist-logged; and it is a marvellous spot for children who do not need organized entertainment. A row of pretty cottages straggles along the shores of Loch Carron, facing one of the most charming views in Scotland. In August there is a yachting regatta. *Strome Ferry 8 km/5 ml.*

PRESTWICK (pop. 13,000), *Ayr./Strathclyde* Port of entry for overseas visitors arriving by air at the international airport, the most fog-free in the British Isles, Prestwick is renowned for its four fine golf courses where many championships have taken place. For children there are all the traditional amusements associated with a seaside town, and the sands are excellent. There are lovely views across the Firth of Clyde to the mountains of Arran.

There are a few interesting old buildings, particularly the ruined **Church of St Nicholas** (1163) and **Kingcase Well** where once stood a lazar house built by Robert the Bruce who is said to have been cured of leprosy here. There is also an ancient Mercat Cross. In a Georgian mansion, **Adamton House,** banquets in 18th-century style are held (commercially) most evenings. *Ayr 5 km/3 ml; Dumfries 98/61; Glasgow 48/30; Largs 50/31.*

ROTHESAY (pop. 7000), *Bute/Strathclyde* Rothesay lies half way down the east coast of the island of Bute which sits in the Kyles (narrows) of Bute, hugging the Argyll coast. Yachting regattas, a cinema, and a pavilion for dancing are some of the attractions of this resort, the first love of Glaswegians who come here in their thousands during the 'Glasgow Fair', the annual Glasgow holiday in the last two weeks of July. This is a town completely given over to tourists, and facilities include three golf courses, five bowling greens, tennis courts, indoor swimming pools, boating and fishing. There is an 11th-century **Castle** surrounded by a water-moat. The entrance is through a high tower which is the work of James IV and James V. The **Bute Museum** will give you information about nature trails on the island—six trails to walk and one for cars.

Rothesay can be reached by steamer from Wemyss Bay (the quickest crossing, and well served by trains from Glasgow), or from several other Clyde towns. A particularly attractive sail is through the Kyles of Bute to Tarbert (Loch Fyne), for the mountains of Argyll sweep down to the water, making this trip really spectacular. *Glasgow 51 km/32 ml (from Wemyss Bay).*

ST ANDREWS (pop. 12,000), *Fife* This ancient Royal Burgh was granted its charter in 1140 by King David, and is the home of Scotland's oldest University (1412) whose students wear striking red gowns. The **Church of St Salvator,** a beautiful 15th-century building, is now the University Chapel, and together with the **Chapel of St Leonard** is one of the few early buildings that still survive. Further down South Street stands **St Mary's College** (1537) where two sides of the quadrangle are formed by the original buildings.

By walking along The Scores, as the promenade is called, the visitor can also see the bathing pools, the ruined Cathedral and the equally ruined Castle. Not much of the 12th- to 14th-century **Cathedral** remains, although it was the largest in Scotland with a nave of 108 m (355 ft). It did not suffer particularly during the Reformation, but it was allowed to fall into bad condition and, in common with so many other fine buildings, was then used as a 'quarry' during the 17th and 18th centuries. Nearby is the small 12th-century **Church of St Rule** with a slender 33 m (108 ft) tower, and there are also several remains of the original monastery.

Elsewhere throughout the town there are fascinating little alleys which are worth exploring, and some of the gracious crescents are equal to the best of those in Georgian Edinburgh. It is, however, as the home of the **Royal and Ancient Golf Club** of St Andrews, the ruling authority of the game, that St Andrews is most widely known, and the Old Course—one of the four full courses at St Andrews—is perhaps the most famous in the world. Some form of golf has probably been played here for 500 years.

In other respects St Andrews is a pleasant seaside resort with fine stretches of sandy beach, a tidal swimming pool, an attractive harbour and the delightful, tiny Byre Theatre. *Callander 103 km/64 ml; Edinburgh 79/49; Perth 50/31; Pitlochry 85/53.*

ST MONANCE See EAST NEUK

SELKIRK (pop. 5636), *Selkirk./ Borders* A mill town, though the industrial evidence is well hidden on the river banks below the main square. There is a statue to Sir Walter Scott in the Market Place, for in the Court House there (now the Town Hall) Sir Walter acted as county sheriff for 33 years. There is also a statue to explorer Mungo Park. Anyone interested in food may like to note that the baker in Market Place is where the now-traditional Selkirk Bannock originated and is still baked (a fruity tea loaf to be spread with butter).

Only in very recent years has **Bowhill,** home of the Scotts of Buccleuch been open to the public. It stands 5 km (3 ml) west of Selkirk, off the A708, and has a very fine art collection. *Galashiels 10 km/6 ml.*

SKYE (pop. 8000), *Inverness./ Highland* One of the major attractions of Scottish tourism, Skye is rarely a disappointment. It is the island around which songs and romantic tales of Bonnie Prince Charlie's flight, disguised as Flora Macdonald's maid, have been woven. Flora Macdonald is buried at **Kilmuir** where a Celtic cross, with lines by Dr Johnson, marks her grave, and she is said to have bid farewell to the Prince in the present *Royal Hotel,* Portree. There is also an interesting craft museum at Kilmuir.

You will need at least three days to see the island from a base like Portree unless, of course, the romance, the mists and the beauty of Skye induce you to stay longer. **Portree** is the capital of the island, and is served by steamer from Mallaig; a busy car ferry runs from Kyle of Lochalsh in only a few minutes to **Kyleakin,** and buses go from Kyleakin via Broadford and Sligachan to Portree, but this small town of sturdy white-washed buildings should really be seen first from the sea. From here you can visit the tiny village of

Elgol, not for the sake of the few tiny scattered cottages and minute post office but for the magnificent view of the **Cuillins,** probably the most dramatic range of mountains in Britain. They should not be climbed by the untrained, for they can be very dangerous, but skilled mountaineers and rock climbers will love them. From Elgol it is worth taking the open boat trip to **Loch Coruisk,** one of the most beautifully set of all Scotland's lochs.

The other main attraction on Skye is **Dunvegan Castle,** home of the chief of the Clan MacLeod. Said to be the oldest continuously inhabited castle in Scotland, it is small and cosy for a castle and contains fascinating relics of the clan and also of Bonnie Prince Charlie. Boat trips from Dunvegan village can often be arranged to see the nearby seal colony. There are several attractive centres on the island, and good roads for the motorist who will always find a good picnicking spot. Here, however, as elsewhere in the Western Highlands, midges can be bothersome, and visitors would be well advised to take some insect repellent with them.

At **Boreraig,** once home of the legendary MacCrimmon family, said to be the greatest pipers in the world, there is a move to establish an international Piping Centre. The aim is to have a constantly updated display of piping information with MacCrimmon music on tape, played by the world's best pipers, and in manuscript form. *From Kyleakin: Dunvegan 76 km/47 ml; Portree 58/36; Sligachan 42/26.*

SPEAN BRIDGE (pop. 150), *Inverness./Highland* Situated 16 km (10 ml) north east of Fort William this village is primarily visited by those who want to see the memorial erected in 1950 to the Commandos of the Second World War, who were trained in the surrounding hills. It stands about 2 km (1 ml) from the bridge just off the Inverness road. Spean Bridge is also a good centre for sporting outdoor holidays.

Nearby is Loch Lochy, one of the three lochs of the **Caledonian Canal** which connects Inverness and Fort William. It was completed in 1847 after 44 years of construction and runs through the magnificent scenery of Glen More. It is still navigable. *Inverness 92 km/57 ml; Mallaig 85/53; Newtonmore 60/37; Oban 95/59.*

STIRLING (pop. 30,000), *Stirling./Central* Towering over this ancient royal burgh, **Stirling Castle** cannot be ignored by the tourist approaching Stirling from the west along the valley of the Forth. It stands on a 110 m (360 ft) rock guarding the Forth-Clyde Valley, and consists of mainly 15th- and 16th-century buildings, although Alexander I died here in 1124, and there must have been fortifications on this spot long before then. The Castle is being restored, but the Palace (1540) is an extraordinary building; the Douglas Room contains some interesting exhibits, and there is a good view from 'Queen Victoria's Lookout'.

Go down the steps from the Castle Esplanade, by a statue of Bruce, to Castle Wynd and **Argyll's Lodging,** a fine 17th-century town house which evokes a period when many noblemen had homes in Stirling—the town has long been associated with the history of Scotland and its leaders. Nearby are the sites of the Battles of Stirling Bridge (1297)—the **Wallace Monument** stands on a hill to the north east—and Bannockburn (1314), where the exhibition centre and the statue of Robert the Bruce by the sculptor, Pilkington Jackson, are worth seeing.

Mary Queen of Scots was crowned in the Church of the Holy Rood which has some attractive 15th-century parts, and in the **Smith Institute** are some local antiquities. The most interesting buildings are close to the Castle hill, but there are many fascinating streets and houses.

Stirling provides golf, tennis, bowls, fishing and boating, and there is a music festival in the spring; the town is a good shopping centre, but most visitors will use Stirling as a touring centre from which to explore further north. An excellent base is provided by the modern **University**, on beautiful Airthrey estate, where student flats in this delightful setting are let to families in the summer (contact the Vacations Letting Officer at the University). The campus also houses the unique Arts complex, the **MacRobert Centre**, which offers to the public an excellent programme ranging from opera and ballet to experimental theatre. *Edinburgh 58 km/36 ml; Glasgow 43/27; Montrose 132/82; Pitlochry 92/57.*

STONEHAVEN (pop. 5000), *Kincardine./Grampian* Although the beach is of pebbles, this town is an excellent seaside resort offering all the traditional pastimes as well as golf, tennis, a large caravan site and a heated open air swimming pool. The attractive pink stone buildings are grouped around the small harbour which

sits in a pleasant curve of the bay, and this area forms the Old Town. The New Town lies to the north of the River Carron. In the Old Town the most interesting building is the Old Tolbooth (16th-century), recently restored and now a teashop and museum.

Dunottar Castle lies 3 km (2 ml) south of Stonehaven standing on a rocky headland that thrusts out into the North Sea. Some of the remains go back to the 14th century, the gate houses date from the latter half of the 16th century. The most impressive views of the castle are from the sea, and boatmen will take you round from Stonehaven.

Crathes Castle dating from the 16th century is open to visitors but on no account should you miss the gardens which are very famous (off A93 5½ km/3½ ml E of Banchory). *Aberdeen 24 km/15 ml; Braemar 85/53; Montrose 35/22.*

STRANRAER (pop. 10,000), *Wigtown./Dumfries and Galloway* Stranraer is known primarily as the terminal of the important passenger and car ferry service to Larne in Northern Ireland, and it is possible to go over to Ireland for a day or so if the attractions of the town—golf, fishing, bathing—pall. The gardens at **Ardwell House**, particularly fine in autumn, are open to the public, Monday to Friday. In the attractive old part of the town there is a 16th-century **Castle**, and **North-West Castle House**, now a hotel, was once the home of Sir John Ross (1777–1856) the Arctic Explorer. It is also a good centre from which to explore Galloway. The Botanic Gardens at **Logan** have many exceptional plants. There is also an unusual fish pond at Logan (23 km/14 ml

S of Stranraer). *Ayr 82 km/51 ml; Carlisle 163/101; Dumfries 111/69; Glasgow 135/84.*

STRATHPEFFER (pop. 850), *Ross and Cromarty/Highland* At one time a fashionable spa, now better known as a touring centre, Strathpeffer lies in a lovely wooded valley and offers golf, fishing, and walking. Nearby Ben Wyvis (1045 m/3429 ft) is not a difficult climb, and a short distance away are the vitrified fort of **Knockfarrel** (296 m/972 ft): good view points from Raven's Rock (266 m/874 ft); and View Rock (152 m/500 ft). See the **Falls of Rogie** on the Blackwater and several lovely lochs. Highland Games are held in the grounds of **Castle Leod** on the first Saturday in August. *Inverness 47 km/29 ml; Kyle of Lochalsh 101/63; Ullapool 66/41.*

TARBERT, Loch Fyne, *Argyll./Strathclyde* The name Tarbert (or Tarbet) means an isthmus over which boats could be dragged; the early sailors who dragged their boats across at Tarbert saved themselves a long sail round the Mull of Kintyre to the Hebrides, etc. Tarbert is in fact two settlements, both small, which have steamer connections with the Clyde on one side and the islands of Islay and Jura on the other. There are the remains of a 14th-century **Castle**, once the home of Robert the Bruce. *Campbeltown 61 km/38 ml; Glasgow 156/97.*

TARBET, Loch Lomond, *Dunbarton./Strathclyde* The lovely village of Tarbet lies at the peaceful end of Loch Lomond. Old cottages are set back from the main road, and some new ones have been built for local North of Scotland Hydro-Electric Board staff. Many houses bear bed and breakfast signs, and there is a large hotel beside the loch. A mecca for tourists on summer weekends, but still an attractive centre with magnificent views of Ben Lomond; Arrochar on Loch Long lies just across the isthmus. A regular steamer service plies up and down Loch Lomond, connecting Tarbet with Balloch station and the trains for Glasgow. At Balloch leave time to see **Cameron House** and grounds. Lots of exhibits here from model aircraft to whisky bottles. *Glasgow 61 km/38 ml; Inveraray 35/22; Lochearnhead 56/35.*

THURSO (pop. 9000), *Caithness/Highland* This most northerly of Scotland's towns has on its doorstep the fast atomic reactor at Dounreay where there is an atomic energy exhibition in summer. The town is now a mixture of old fishermen's houses, many of which face away from the strong sea winds, some pleasant Georgian houses and much new building. The Thurso River runs through the town and is known for its fine fishing. There are fine sandy beaches and all along this northern coast one can find deserted sandy bays—a wonderful area for those who like the great outdoors. Between Thurso and **John o'Groats** lies the **Castle of Mey** (19 km/12 ml), holiday home of the Queen Mother, with beautiful gardens open to the public three days a year. *Durness 130 km/81 ml; Inverness 196/122; John o'Groats 32/20; Ullapool 195/121.*

TIREE and **COLL** (pop. 1100), *Argyll./Western Isles* **Coll,** 11 km (7 ml) west of Mull is largely agricultural with a rocky east coast and fine sandy bays on the west, the main attraction along with the fishing for brown trout in the lochs, for visitors to the hotel at **Arinagour.** Coll is reached by steamer from Oban.

Close by is **Tiree,** also served by the Oban steamer and with the added facility of a regular air service from Glasgow, and a small golf course.

This is essentially a flat, agricultural island (the ideal way to get around the island is by bicycle) but the mild climate has made possible the cultivation of daffodil and tulip bulbs in recent years, in addition to the traditional occupation of fishing.

TROON (pop. 11,600), *Ayr./ Strathclyde* A small douce resort with good beaches, and a mecca for golfers since there are several good golf courses nearby. The ruined castle of **Dundonald** dates back to the 13th century. *Ayr 10 km/6 ml.*

ULLAPOOL (pop. 600), *Ross and Cromarty/Highland* There is something immensely reassuring about the trim, clean little houses stacked in a few rows around the curve of Loch Broom after a long drive through the silent mountain roads from Dingwall. This bustling village was founded in 1788 by the Fisheries Association and this is still an important industry, although at the height of the season tourism tends to take over—understandably, for this is one of the most beautiful villages of the west coast, and one of the outstanding scenes of the Highlands is a fiery red sunset over Loch Broom with the fishing boats returning home.

The street names are given in both Gaelic and English, an odd touch which gives this remote village a very businesslike air. Almost every cottage offers tourist accommodation and there are several hotels. Visitors can fish, swim, walk, stalk and take boat trips to the uninhabited **Summer Isles.** There is a bus service from Lairg (89 km/55 ml).

At **Braemore** (19 km/12 ml SSE of Ullapool) it is worth seeing the Corrieshalloch Gorge from the suspension bridge viewpoint. The gorge is 2 km (1 ml) long and 60 m (200 ft) deep. *Dornoch 100 km/62 ml; Glasgow 348/216; Inverness 93/58.*

WICK (pop. 7557), *Caithness/ Highland* Reached by rail, road, plane and steamer, Wick is the most important communications centre with the north and the isles of Orkney and Shetland. It is also a commercial fishing centre, and in the herring season (July to September) the harbour is the centre of attraction.

There is a golf course (18-hole, 5 km/3 ml away), a swimming pool, good angling in the Wick and nearby lochs, and tennis courts. This is a brisk and interesting town—the old Town Hall is most attractive—in an area of magnificent cliff scenery dotted with historic castles such as **Sinclair** and **Girnigoe** and the 14th-century Castle of Old Wick of which a solitary tower remains, known as the **Old Man of Wick** (2 km/1¼ ml south). Caithness glass, sold all over the country and commended by the Design Centre for its clean 'Scandinavian' (!) lines, is manufactured here. *John o'Groats 27 km/17 ml; Lairg 103/64; Thurso 34/21.*

INDEX

All places which have a main entry and the pages on which they occur are printed in heavy type. Asterisks denote illustrations. Map references are printed in italics.